Cummings

KENNETH BAKER

The Prime Ministers

*An Irreverent Political History
in Cartoons*

WITH 209 ILLUSTRATIONS
46 IN COLOUR

THAMES AND HUDSON

Dedicated to the memory of my father,
Wilfred Baker, and his pithy Welsh scepticism

Illustration Acknowledgments

Kenneth Baker Collection 2; 27; 33; 35 (t. and b.); 37; 38; 40; 42 (t.l. and t.r.); 46; 47; 49; 50; 51 (t.); 52; 53; 55; 57; 60; 61; 62 (m. and b.); 63; 65; 66 (t. and b.); 67; 69; 70; 71; 72; 73; 74 (t.); 75 (t. and b.); 77; 79; 80; 81 (t.); 82; 83 (t. and b.); 84; 85 (t. and b.); 86 (t. and b.); 87; 88; 89; 90 (t. and b.); 91; 118; 122; 123; 124 (b.); 125; 126; 127; 133 (t.); 134 (b.); 135; 137. Max Beerbohm (courtesy Beerbohm Estate) 15; 129; 131; 138; 139 (t. and b.); 159 (t.). Steve Bell 180 (b.); 185; 186 (b.). Birmingham Reference Library 134 (t.). Trustees of the British Museum, London 9; 21; 22; 23; 25; 26; 28; 31; 32 (t.); 32 (b.); 34; 39; 41; 42 (b.); 43; 44; 45 (t. and b.); 51 (b.); 56; 81 (b.). Peter Brookes 187. Cartoon Study Centre, University of Kent 5; 14; 16 (l.); 145; 153 (t.); 154; 155 (b.); 167 (t. and b.); 170 (b.); 173 (t.); 177 (b.); 181 (t.). Michael Cummings 1; 18–19. Andrew Edmunds 59; 64 (l. and r.); 76. Express Newspapers plc: Cummings 161; 162 (b.); 168 (b.); 173 (b.); 182 (t.); Giles 170 (t.); Osbert Lancaster 158 (b.); Strube 147; 150 (b.); 152; 153 (t.); 158 (t.l.). Nicholas Garland 181. Les Gibbard 177 (t.); 182 (b.). House of Commons Library 62 (t.); 74 (b.); 119; 121; 124 (t.); 128. *The Independent*: Heath 19 (b.). Kal 183 (b.). John Kent 172; 174. Ewan MacNaughton Associates, © *The Telegraph* plc, London, 1995: Garland 186 (t.); Jensen 173 (t.); 177 (b.). *Private Eye* 183 (t.); 188 (t.). *Punch*: Illingworth 162 (t.); 164 (t.); 165 (t. and b.); 168 (t.); E.H. Shepard 153 (b.); Trog 175. Chris Riddell (*Economist*) 189. Gerald Scarfe 169; 171; 176; 184 (b.). Ronald Searle 163. Solo Syndication & Literary Agency: Low 14; 145; 151; 154; 155 (b.); 157; 160; 164 (b.); Mac 188 (b.); Vicky 16 (l.); 159 (b.); 167 (t. and b.); 170 (b.). Ralph Steadman 16 (r.); 181 (t.). Trog 180 (t.). Richard Willson 179.

Special photography by La Belle Aurore (Juliet Coombe and Steve Davey).

Key t. = top; t.l. = top left; t.r. = top right; m. = middle; b. = bottom; l. = left; r. = right

HALF-TITLE PAGE
Cummings cartoon of Margaret Thatcher and Edward Heath.
FRONTISPIECE
Away with him! Tom Merry depicts politicians of all parties
uniting to kick Gladstone out after his Government's defeat on the
Irish Home Rule Bill, 1886.
CONTENTS PAGE
Vicky on the brilliantly versatile Winston Churchill.

British Library Cataloguing-in-Publication Data

A catalogue record for this book is available from the British
Library.

ISBN 0-500-01679-8

Printed and bound in Slovenia by Mladinska Knjiga

CONTENTS

Preface

THIS BOOK developed from two programmes that I made for the BBC in 1994, 'From Walpole's Bottom to Major's Underpants'. I would like to thank the BBC, the Director of the programmes, Anne Tyerman, the Producer, Alison Cahn, and the Assistant Producer, Rabinder Minhas, for all their help.

I would also like to thank most warmly Roy Douglas for the assistance he has given me in producing the book. Roy, who has stood for the Liberals in five Parliamentary elections, describes himself as a semi-retired academic, but he continues to teach political history at Surrey University. He has written several excellent books himself on history as seen through cartoons, the most recent being *Great Nations Still Enchained* and *The Great War 1914–18, The Cartoonists' Vision*. He was particularly helpful to me in checking facts and dates throughout, but he does not necessarily agree with all the judgments. I am especially grateful to him for finding cartoons in German, French and Russian periodicals.

In addition, I would like to thank the historian, Rosemary Baker, who is compiling the Index for the first five volumes of the British Museum's catalogue of personal and social satires. I was very glad to be able to call upon her voluminous knowledge of the early prints. My gratitude also goes to Anthony Griffiths, the Keeper of the Print Room at the British Museum, his deputy, Martin Royalton-Kisch, and their staff for their friendly enthusiasm in helping me examine their large collection of prints, as well as their permission to include many of them in this book.

Among other thanks, I must include Andrew Edmunds, of the Andrew Edmunds Gallery, 44 Lexington Street, London W1R 3LH. He is the doyen of the trade in 18th- and 19th-Century political prints and gave his permission to include three from his own collection. I also thank Chris Beetles, of the Chris Beetles Art Gallery, 8 Ryder Street, London SW1Y 6QB, himself the doyen of late 19th- and 20th-Century political drawings and cartoons, for his comments and his help in providing several transparencies.

My warm thanks go to Amanda-Jane Doran, the Curator of the *Punch* Library, for drawing upon her knowledge of *Punch*'s significant contribution to British cartoon art, and to Jane Newton, Assistant

Director of the University of Kent's Centre for the Study of Cartoons and Caricature at The Templeman Library, for her permission to include several cartoons from their collection. This Centre has an important and growing collection of 20th-Century and contemporary cartoons. Its computer-based catalogue is outstanding and an example to other libraries.

I was also lucky to be able to draw upon the great knowledge and enthusiasm of Simon Heneage, who has the finest collection of cartoons in private hands in the country.

May I also thank all the following for their permission to include cartoons from their collections or estates: Jeffrey Archer for five cartoons from his growing collection; the Piccadilly Gallery for a Beerbohm cartoon of Balfour; the Cartoon Art Trust for a Trog cartoon of Ted Heath; *Private Eye* for three cartoons; *Spitting Image* for one; the Executors or Estates of Max Beerbohm, Strube, David Low, Vicky, Illingworth and Osbert Lancaster; Malcolm Hay, the Curator of Works of Art in the House of Commons, for making available some 18th- and 19th-Century cartoons from the House of Commons; and the Librarian of the House of Lords, Mr D.L. Jones, for his permission to use some of the Gillrays in their fine collections.

My appreciation and gratitude goes to the following contemporary cartoonists: Steve Bell, Peter Brookes, Michael Cummings, Wally Fawkes (Trog), Nicholas Garland, Les Gibbard, Michael Heath, Jensen, Kal, John Kent, Stan McMurtry, Chris Riddell, Gerald Scarfe, Ronald Searle, Ralph Steadman and Richard Willson. Finally, thanks to La Belle Aurore (Juliet Coombe and Steve Davey) for their skilled photography of many of the cartoons.

I have tried to find the owners of the copyright of all the cartoons that I have included, but some have proved elusive. I would welcome any assistance in tracing them.

KENNETH BAKER
April 1995

Introduction

POLITICAL CARTOONS and the office of Prime Minister both became established in the 1720s. They grew alongside each other and established a strange relationship which was to show itself in mutual interdependence as it developed over the next two and a half centuries.

In this book I have called the leading minister in each administration the 'Prime Minister', although the title only came into general use in the 19th Century. In the 18th Century, the leading minister usually held the post of First Lord of the Treasury, as Walpole did. He did not use the title Prime Minister, though to attack his powerful position, his opponents did. Twenty years after his fall, the leading minister was Chatham. While he was not even First Lord of the Treasury, he was clearly the leading minister in a Government nominally led by the Duke of Newcastle. It was, however, Chatham's son, William Pitt, in his long premiership from 1784 to 1801, who really established the institution of Prime Minister. After that, the leading minister of the Crown was clearly the Prime Minister.

The word 'cartoon' as a generic description of satirical attacks upon politicians came into general use in the 19th Century. Before that, the cartoons appeared as individual prints which were etched or engraved and sold as separate items. Gillray started to produce his prints from the early 1780s and I have used the word 'print' to describe those that appeared before then, 'cartoon' for those that appeared after.

Some prints and cartoons are also caricatures and here a further definition is needed. The art of caricature began in Italy in the late 17th Century. Deriving its name from Annibale Carracci, it was first popularized in Rome by P. L. Ghezzi (1674–1755). Sarah, the great Duchess of Marlborough, had heard about these amusing and scurrilous drawings of well-known Italian figures. She said to one of her friends, 'Young man, you come from Italy. They tell me of the new invention called caricatura drawing. Can you find me somebody that will make me a caricature of Lady Masham, describing her covered with many sores and ulcers, that I may send to the Queen to give her a slight idea of her favourite?'

A caricature is like a distorting mirror. It exaggerates physical characteristics to delineate character. It usually stands alone as a drawing of one person, like Hogarth's famous engraving of John Wilkes. In this book, there are several caricatures: Walpole's Bottom is one, and so is

Sir Robert Walpole, the first Prime Minister.

Pitt's Darning Needle, Beerbohm's Balfour and Gerald Scarfe's Thatcher. These do not depend upon any particular incident; they are the summation of many acts, speeches and appearances.

Cartoons, on the other hand, usually deal with a particular event. They are drawn immediately after something has happened. Subsequently, they usually need some explanation, for the exact memory of the events may well have faded. If a cartoonist has been successful in establishing a caricature of his target as a recognizable image, then he will often use that caricature in the cartoon. This is true of Steve Bell, for example, who created the caricature of John Major as a naff Superman, wearing his underpants over his trousers. In Bell's strip cartoons, John Major is now regularly depicted in that mode.

The Eighteenth Century

In the third decade of the 18th Century, William Hogarth started to draw and sell his engravings of social matters – *A Harlot's Progress* (1730–32), *The Rake's Progress* (*c.* 1733) and *Marriage à la Mode* (*c.* 1753). These were bought by people who could not afford paintings, but wanted some decoration for their houses. Their success encouraged others to produce engravings and a new, popular fashion in art had begun.

Just before this, Robert Walpole became the King's leading Minister. Later, he came to live at No. 10 Downing Street – a house given to him by George II, so that he could be close to the Court and to Parliament.

He sustained his position as head of the Government by maintaining, through his use of Royal patronage, a majority in the House of Commons. Only when he lost that majority in 1742 did he have to leave office.

Walpole was a political giant and that is what the engraver and etcher of the prints needed. He was the first major political figure to be attacked in prints and it says much for the courage of the largely unknown engravers that they dared to fire their darts at the most powerful man in England.

It is significant that the earliest prints appeared at a time when Walpole was very unpopular. In 1733, he tried to introduce a broad-based Excise Tax – somewhat similar to VAT today – and he is depicted as a bullying dictator imposing a bad tax upon the people. He was also depicted as a Colossus with feet of clay; as a corrupt seller of Government jobs; and – most famously – as a naked bottom straddling the Treasury, for if you wanted to get on in the early 18th Century you had – at least metaphorically – to kiss Walpole's bottom.

Such attacks in visual form were novel and unusual. Walpole objected, and he responded by having some of the print sellers arrested and held for a few days. But he was not able to control prints in the same way as he controlled plays, which he considered to be more subversive. Accordingly, he introduced theatre censorship, which was to survive until the 1950s. Instead of attempting to suppress prints, Walpole decided to create his own propaganda. He commissioned prints showing him as a great statesman – the first example of a Prime Minister playing the media game. In 1741, when his enemies were gathering, Walpole's friends had a print produced showing the collapse of the opposition. His opponents were stung to respond by publishing a print attacking his corruption. So even by the 1740s, prints had become a way of continuing and extending the political battle.

The prints were produced in quite small quantities for the political and social elite of London. They circulated in the coffee houses of St James's, Pall Mall, Piccadilly, the Strand and the City. But they were not cheap. The price of a print was roughly equivalent to a month's supply of candles – so prints, like candles, were bought by the better off. The few people who saw them had influence in political, financial, or Court circles; prints could not be ignored by those in the 'know'. The engravers of the prints were usually anonymous, though – by law – the printseller had to put his name and address at the bottom of each print. Some of the finest prints of Walpole were drawn by George Bickham, and some carried his name. He can fairly be described as Britain's first political cartoonist.

Even at this early stage, the elements of the Prime Minister/cartoonist relationship were being fashioned and were becoming recognizable. The cartoonists needed a hate figure who was an identifiable public enemy; Walpole was the first. Because Walpole so overshadowed his ministerial colleagues, the 'Prime Minister' became the symbol of the administration. It was Walpole's Government, just as later it was to be Gladstone's, or Margaret Thatcher's.

After Walpole's fall, the cartoonists were at a loss because the other politicians were pygmies. The greatest insult for a Prime Minister was to be ignored. No print exists of Waldegrave who, in 1757, was the Prime Minister for ten days; and only one exists of the Duke of Devonshire, who survived for six months. Walpole's immediate successor, the Earl of Wilmington, only appears in two prints, although he held office as First Lord of the Treasury for eighteen months. The length of time in office, however, did not necessarily matter. In 1827, Canning and Goderich were both Prime Ministers for a few months, but as Canning was the bigger figure there are many cartoons featuring him, while those of Goderich are rare. Cartoonists need big figures.

The golden age of British cartooning was from 1780 to 1830. The images created by James Gillray, Thomas Rowlandson, James Sayers, Richard Newton, Isaac Cruikshank, William Dent, George Cruikshank and William Heath, of the Prime Ministers, Lord North, Pitt the Younger, Addington, Grenville of the Broad Bottom, Liverpool, Canning and Wellington are very much how these Prime Ministers have been remembered by succeeding generations.

The 18th Century was a period of violence and sexual explicitness, and the cartoons reflect this. Defecation, urination and fornication appear frequently. In one cartoon, of the extraordinary coalition of North and Fox in 1783, the two partners are shown defecating into a common pot, which the devil is stirring. Shelburne, Prime Minister for six months in 1782, suffered the indignity of having his male member shown. William Pitt the Younger was depicted as being blind drunk, which he quite often was.

In the 18th Century, prints and cartoons were the way in which politicians came to be recognized by a wider public. Most people in the country could not read: most would never have seen a leading politician. By 1780, there were several print shops in central London, which employed artists to etch or engrave an impression of the current political crisis. The engravers cut their images into copper plates, which were then inked: several hundred impressions were run off within a day and hung up for sale in the print-shop windows. Gillray usually coloured the first impression and left it to others to copy his colouring. In this way, the world of politics was available visually, not just to the inner circle of the educated middle class, but to anyone who passed the print shop, or saw them in the coffee houses. This more popular art required heroes and villains.

The wider recognition helped to enhance the position of the Prime Minister. It actually helped William Pitt the Younger to be featured so many times, for he was the leader of the nation locked into war with revolutionary France. So important were these prints that the friends of Pitt were alarmed when Gillray portrayed him as a drunkard or as a tyrant trampling upon the ancient liberties of all free Englishmen. They decided that they must get Gillray on their side. Canning, a young friend of Pitt, and later himself to be a Prime Minister, probably had a hand in arranging for a pension to be paid to Gillray from 1797. After that date, Pitt was presented in a much more favourable light. When Pitt left office in 1801, as George III would not support his proposals on Catholic emancipation, he is shown as a noble figure – *Integrity Retiring from Office*. This print was given to Margaret Thatcher when she was forced from office in 1990.

The Victorian Age

From 1820, political woodcuts were added to news sheets and pamphlets, and the need for individual prints began to dwindle. Newspapers not only killed the tradition of the print shop, they also suppressed the vigour and scurrility of the 18th Century. Editors did not want to shock their readers, who were very sensitive about exposing their wives and children to crudity and vulgarity. Middle-class morality had taken over. As a result, Prime Ministers from Grey in 1830 to Asquith in 1914 had a much easier ride than their predecessors. They were not portrayed with naked bottoms, defecating, urinating or fornicating, they were depicted as statesmen. Their policies and judgments were criticized, but they were not usually subjected to withering personal ridicule.

Satirical magazines, such as *The Looking Glass* and *Figaro*, appeared in the 1830s, while *Punch* was first published in 1841. *Punch* reinforced the trend; it also created the weekly political cartoon, which was meant to sum up the nation's feelings about the latest political crisis. The cartoons by John Leech and Sir John Tenniel were intended to approve, or

Victorian benevolence: Tenniel on Disraeli.

occasionally to reprove, but always to improve. Disrespect was banished. The humour became wordier, with many literary and classical allusions. The aggressive insult was bleached out of the cartoon, but intensified in the politician's rhetoric. The spoken words hurled at each other by Disraeli and Gladstone were more wounding than the cartoons of Tenniel and Leach.

Cartoonists also liked striking physical characteristics – Peel was too bland, Aberdeen was too flat, Rosebery too smooth. They much preferred Russell because he was so short; Palmerston because he was so jaunty, with a wisp of straw in the corner of his mouth; Disraeli for his Jewish oriental appearance; and Gladstone for his high-minded solemnity, which summed up the strength of Victorian England.

Following *Punch*, a large number of other magazines sprang up – *Judy, Fun, The Tomahawk, Will-o'the-Wisp* and *Funny Folk*. All carried political cartoons, some pro-Liberal, some pro-Conservative. They all helped to make the major political figures nationally recognized. From the 1870s, photography was also to fulfil that role, but the popularity of the magazines survived because the electorate wanted political comment and not just exact representation. Right up to the end of the century, the cartoonists respected the politicians. Francis Carruthers Gould, who was a Liberal supporter, did not savage Salisbury. Harry Furniss's drawings of

Gladstone, wearing high wing collars and in a frenzy of debate, were really a tribute to the Grand Old Man. It is impossible to find an unfriendly cartoon of Campbell-Bannerman.

The Twentieth Century

The age of cartoon deference came to an end with Max Beerbohm. With delicious irony and exquisite economy of line, he made Prime Ministers figures of fun. In his subtle, delicate way, he reintroduced ridicule. A contemporary of his, Will Dyson, a cartoonist from Australia, reintroduced anger. He drew for the *Herald*, a Labour newspaper, and he attacked the establishment, whether Tory or Liberal. The young Ramsay MacDonald, who was the Chairman of the emerging Labour Party, was attacked for wanting to compromise with the Liberal Party. There was a distinct sharpening of comment, which was temporarily suspended for the duration of the First World War.

After the War, it became common for newspapers to carry regular, daily cartoons since they helped to sell the papers. The greatest patron of cartooning was Lord Beaverbrook, who employed – at the *Daily Express* and the *Evening Standard* – two of the greatest 20th-Century cartoonists – David Low and Vicky – as well as many others, like Strube, Osbert Lancaster and Michael Cummings. Beaverbrook did not care that Low and Vicky were well to the left and he never censored any of their cartoons.

In the 1930s, day after day, David Low took on Stanley Baldwin and Neville Chamberlain in the *Evening Standard* for their appeasement of Mussolini and Hitler. It has to be recognized, however, that the country remained broadly supportive of their appeasement policies, but that did not deter Low. Even when Chamberlain was feted on his return from Munich, Low still portrayed him as weak, misguided and wrong.

Low's unequivocal view of Chamberlain and appeasement, 1939.

Max Beerbohm's parade of Prime Ministers, from Disraeli to Baldwin.

Cartoonists are not always pitched against the prevailing mood of the country. Yet one of their duties is not to conform and, in this case, Low was justified by history.

Cartoonists do like their targets to have props by which they can be recognized. The prop becomes the shorthand for the Prime Minister. For Walpole it was the Ribbon of the Garter, which he wore when he was hunting and when he went to the House of Commons, giving him the name 'Sir Blue String'; for Neville Chamberlain, it was the umbrella; for Churchill, the cigar; for Harold Wilson, the pipe; and for Margaret Thatcher, the handbag. Indeed, Prime Ministers have lived up to their images. In his television interviews, Harold Wilson spent more time playing with his pipe than actually smoking it. Margaret Thatcher seemed never to be without her handbag, though there are many women politicians who are rarely seen carrying one. The Thatcher handbag became the symbol of her authority. It was her sceptre.

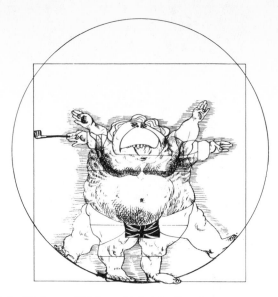

The two Harolds: Macmillan (left) by Vicky and Wilson (right) by Steadman.

Postwar

In the 1960s, there was a re-birth of more savage political satire. Thirteen years of Conservative rule provided an opportunity, but there was also a change in the Spirit of the Times. Deference was definitely out; the Beatles and Rock'n'Roll in: the violent political demonstration returned with a vengeance. The magazine, *Private Eye*, and the television programme, *That Was The Week That Was*, were caustic and disrespectful; they set out to ridicule the high, the mighty and the rich. Cartoon art was in the van of this new sharper age. Gerald Scarfe and Ralph Steadman brought back into cartooning the sharp and vicious scurrility of 18th-Century caricature. Gross distortion returned and bare bottoms were certainly back. Scarfe and Steadman, who seemed angry, sought to destroy: their first victims were Harold Wilson and Ted Heath. Ralph Steadman has said of his portrayal of politicians that he wanted to 'perpetrate a violence'. He succeeded. Today, however, Steadman has abandoned political caricature, because he believes that it encourages politicians. Contemptuous neglect is the best way to cut politicians down to size.

Over the last thirty years, some cartoonists have become a good deal harsher. Their cartoons are cruder, coarser and crueller. This, perhaps, reflects changes in what their readers want to see, or at least what they have grown accustomed to. *Spitting Image* built upon the work of Scarfe and Steadman and introduced political caricature to a much wider audience. It has positively rejected subtlety or wit, preferring violence and gross caricature. But after the target, whether Margaret Thatcher or President Reagan, has been bludgeoned to death, or had his or her brains spilt out and face smashed in, there is not much more you can say or do. Fashions in satire and caricature change and *Spitting Image*'s heyday is over. Most cartoonists today use a more traditional manner, preferring a gentler form of irony and subtle satire. One thing is clear in cartoon history: no new fashion lasts for ever.

Cartoonists and Prime Ministers

In making a judgment about a Prime Minister, cartoonists have certain advantages over political writers or journalists. They can go further in making a sharp comment, knowing that it is well-nigh impossible for a cartoonist to be sued for libel. A visual image can be more memorable than a phrase or a measured political judgment: a political cartoon is visual invective. By being witty, amusing and acerbic, the cartoonist is using humour to great effect: it is laughter that can ruffle the mighty.

From the start, cartoonists and Prime Ministers have needed each other. Michael Cummings, the contemporary cartoonist, has said that a Prime Minister to a cartoonist is as bricks to a builder – 'Without Prime Ministers we'd all be redundant.' It was so from the very start. Similarly, politicians need cartoonists, for to be caricatured is a sign that they have arrived.

It is not surprising that Prime Ministers have liked to be depicted in a favourable light and they can be very resentful if they are presented as figures of ridicule. Several of them have also liked to collect cartoons of themselves. Both Pitt and Fox bought the occasional print; Robert Peel amassed a large collection, which was eventually sold to an American library. Ted Heath has a small collection featuring himself. All depict him favourably. When asked why he did not have any that were critical, he said with an air of aloof dismissal: 'I can't think of any. If they were unfair, I would not remember them.'

As a general rule Prime Ministers have received more criticism than praise from cartoonists. There are a few exceptions. The first was the Elder Pitt, the Earl of Chatham, who was a national hero who had led Britain to victory against France and established the first British Empire. He is generally portrayed favourably and those prints criticizing him were probably commissioned by his rivals. When he succumbed to a state close to madness, the engravers forbore to use their etching needles to depict his sad decline.

Attlee to Major by Cummings.

The second was Churchill. In his early career, he was often the butt of strong attacks. But in the late 1930s, because of his vigorous opposition to appeasement, he became the favourite of the great cartoonist, David Low, although Low was himself a socialist. During the Second World War, cartoonists bolstered Churchill, for the real villains were Hitler and Mussolini.

The third was Margaret Thatcher. She was the subject of many virulent cartoons, but they frequently played to her strength. Cartoons often depicted her as an Iron Lady; or as a strong and determined leader who would not make any U-turns; or as the Prime Minister who wore the trousers. These were rather flattering images. Few cartoonists dented her reputation, though Steve Bell tried to by portraying her as demented. Margaret Thatcher was not affected by these savage cartoons. They never got to her – probably because she never saw them, and she did not watch *Spitting Image*.

Cartoonists do want to draw blood and in some cases they have been successful. One Prime Minister who was clearly rattled by the spate of savage cartoons that appeared in 1761 was Bute: he lost his nerve and left office after a year. Some of his successors have also been sensitive about the intensity of the satirical attacks. Baldwin thought Low was 'evil and malicious'. Anthony Eden used to ring up his Chief Whip, Ted Heath, every morning at 8 o'clock to complain about how the press was treating him.

One of the lessons of this cartoon history is that it does not pay for Prime Ministers to be too sensitive. The Duke of Wellington was seen to laugh at some of the cartoons which featured him, but he was stung by some of them. He said sadly but wisely to his companion, 'There is nothing but calumny in the world, Mrs Arbuthnot, and I must make up my mind to be exposed to it.' At the end of his long political life, Gladstone was cartooned as a crazy old fool. But there is no record of these attacks ruffling his supreme self-confidence. He knew ultimately he had to answer to God, not the British press.

Even the most acerbic prints of Robert Walpole somehow enhanced his reputation by recognizing that he was 'the big man' in British politics. That is not the case for many lesser figures. The Pelhams are embedded for ever in a mire of corruption; Addington is remembered as a pip-squeak; Aberdeen as an old woman; Balfour as a willowy question mark; Eden as a sheep in wolf's clothing.

The conclusion that I would draw from this cartoon history is that the lesser figures can be hurt, particularly if they show that the attack has struck home. But the reputation of the real political giants has not been impaired by the images left by the cartoonist. Great Prime Ministers rise above the invective, no doubt sufficiently confident about their own reputations to allow the Muse of History, rather than the cartoonist, to judge their achievements.

'Is there anything that you think could be worrying you at the moment?'

Heath's John Major, *from* The Independent, *1991.*

1 · Walpole

Sir Robert Walpole, later Earl of Orford
First Lord of the Treasury *21 April 1721–February 1742*

WHEN QUEEN ANNE DIED in 1714, the strongest claimant to the throne on the hereditary principle was Anne's half-brother, James Stuart. He would have become James III, but he had been excluded from the throne by an Act of Parliament passed a decade and a half earlier, because he was a Roman Catholic. The Act also laid down that the Crown should pass to the ruling House of Hanover. The Hanoverian head at that time was the Electress Sophia, a granddaughter of James I, but as she died shortly before Queen Anne, her son, George, succeeded to the throne.

George's greatest asset was that he was not a Catholic. He had an unattractive personality, never becoming popular and showing more interest in his possessions in Hanover than in Britain. Spending much of his time in Germany, he never bothered to learn English properly and conversed or corresponded with his ministers in French or Latin. He was on exceedingly bad terms with his wife, whom he imprisoned. He brought over two ugly mistresses, one tall, thin and dubbed 'The Maypole', who became the Duchess of Kendal, and the other short, fat and dubbed 'The Elephant and Castle', who became the Countess of Darlington.

THE STATUE OF A GREAT MAN, OR, THE ENGLISH COLOSSUS, 1740

Walpole was truly a Colossus that bestrode the world, and he revelled in one of his nicknames, 'The Great Man'. This print by George Bickham sold for sixpence, and appears to depict Walpole as a great man; but it is really an ironic attack upon the latter years of his premiership. Walpole believed in peace and lower taxes; he had no enthusiasm, therefore, for fighting

Spain in the War of Jenkins's Ear, which started in 1739. Indeed, he said that the war began with people ringing the bells and would end with them wringing their hands. This attitude did not please the public, and particularly the merchants of the City of London. So around the feet of the Colossus there is chaos and despair – the fleet cannot sail because not enough ships have been built; one ship is sinking; the sailors are unpaid; the City merchants are deploring the loss of trade; and a bulldog of the true breed 'lies at rest'.

20

The Stature of a

Great Man or the English Coloſſus.

Why Man, he doth bestride ye narrow World | *Men at some times are Masters of their fates:*
like a Coloſsus, and we petty Men — | *The fault, dear P— —y is not in our Stars,*
Walk under his huge Legs, & peep about | *But in our Selves, that we are Underlings—*
To find our Selves, dishonourable Graves. | *Shakespear.*

It was an inauspicious beginning for the Hanoverian dynasty, but George and his successors were saved by the incompetence of the Jacobites, who launched a badly planned and unsuccessful revolt in 1715. Queen Anne had appointed her own ministers and presided over the Cabinet Council. George continued to appoint ministers, but his lack of English and his frequent absences abroad made it impossible for him to play an active role in government, if indeed he had ever cared to do so.

EXCISE IN TRIUMPH, 1733

The general view in the 18th Century was that it was better to tax the poor, since it would encourage them to work. Accordingly, Walpole had favoured repeal of the Candle Tax, since it was paid by the upper and middle classes, and reintroduction of the Salt Tax, which everyone paid. In 1733, he proposed to reduce the Land Tax, which was paid by 400,000 people out of 8 million, and to introduce an Excise Tax on tobacco and wine to replace the import duties,

which were largely avoided by smuggling. This was greeted by a pamphlet and cartoon war in which his opponents claimed that the Excise Duty was going to be applied to everything – just like Value Added Tax today. Although Walpole managed to get a majority of 60 for the First Reading of the Bill, he had to drop it a month later.

This is the most famous print generated by these events. It shows Walpole preparing to introduce his new tax – even if the Army had to thrust it down the throat of the people.

In a second cartoon, the gold from the Excise Duty is shown as flowing into Walpole's lap. Several hawkers were arrested for selling this seditious libel and were brought before a magistrate – though later discharged.

'See this dragon Excise
Has ten thousand Eyes
And Five Thousand Mouths to
devour us
A sting and sharp Claws
With wide-gaping Jaws
And a belly as big as a storehouse.'

In 1715 George appointed Robert Walpole as First Commissioner, or First Lord of the Treasury – a post which he held for 18 months. No one at that time described him as Prime Minister. In 1721 he was recalled to the Treasury to deal with the aftermath of the great financial scandal and panic known as the South Sea Bubble. This time he was to remain in office for nearly 21 years.

In some ways Walpole was a surprising choice. Unlike most important statesmen of the day, he was not an aristocrat, merely a local squire without great wealth. But he sat in the House of Commons and that was the source of his power. For the first nine years Walpole had to assert his authority because other politicians like his brother-in-law, Charles Townshend, were considered equally, or more, important. By 1730 he had emerged as the dominant minister in the Government and he soon began to be described unofficially as 'Prime Minister'.

Walpole had considerable difficulty in keeping office after the death of George I in 1727. George II, like most Hanoverian heirs, was on bad terms with his father and was at first disposed to remove Walpole. Walpole hung on to office by proposing excessively generous payments in the Civil List for the new King and Queen. They knew that only Walpole would be able to get these proposals through the House of Commons – he was indispensable. Walpole had also cultivated the new Queen, Caroline, and was to use her as a means of influencing the King – or, as he put it in his characteristically earthy manner, 'I had the right sow by the ear.' When Caroline died in 1737, Walpole's authority was gradually sapped, but several years were to elapse before he was driven from office.

Walpole's overriding aims were to consolidate the Hanoverian dynasty and its Protestant succession; to avoid war and foreign adventures; and, as a consequence, to reduce taxes. His policy has been dubbed as 'letting sleeping dogs lie', but this underestimates his extraordinary adroitness at handling a succession of very difficult problems.

During his long period in office Walpole built up his own importance, the importance of his job and the importance of the House of Commons. The key to Walpole's hold on office was the exercize of the Crown's patronage, in Parliament, the Church, the Navy and the Army. Nowhere was that patronage more effective than in the management of the House of Commons. In the 18th Century most constituencies were under the domination of a few individuals and frequently only one. Elections were the exception rather than the rule. Where they did occur, the Government's influence was overwhelming – not once in the 18th Century did a Government lose a General Election. Government influence meant essentially the influence that the King exerted personally or through his chosen Ministers by manipulating the massive wealth of the Crown and the power to make innumerable appointments. It was this influence that Walpole wielded so cleverly.

IDOL-WORSHIP, 1740

The most famous print of Walpole was not of his face but of his bottom. Walpole's great naked bottom straddles the entrance to the Treasury and, as the caption says: 'whosoever went out, or whosoever came in, passed beneath, and with idolatrous reverence lift up their eyes and kissed the cheeks of the postern'. On the path of preferment to the Treasury a man drives a hoop inscribed with Wealth, Pride, Vanity, Folly, Luxury, Want, Dependence, Servility, Venality, Corruption and Prostitution.

The passage through to the Treasury Building led from the Parade in St James's Park to Downing Street. It was very important for Walpole to be right at the centre of things and as close as possible to Westminster and the Court of St James. In 1737 he was given No. 10 Downing Street by George II. However, No. 10 had been jerry-built by a property speculator, George Downing, and required a lot of work to put it in good order. Walpole was not prepared to take it over until the Treasury had paid. It became the official residence of the First Lord of the Treasury and the brass plate which is still fixed on the door today carries that title.

Although this drawing bears no particularly distinguishing features of Walpole, all those who saw it knew who it was. In a way it flatters Walpole, since it recognizes his power at the very centre of royal patronage. A big man has a big bottom.

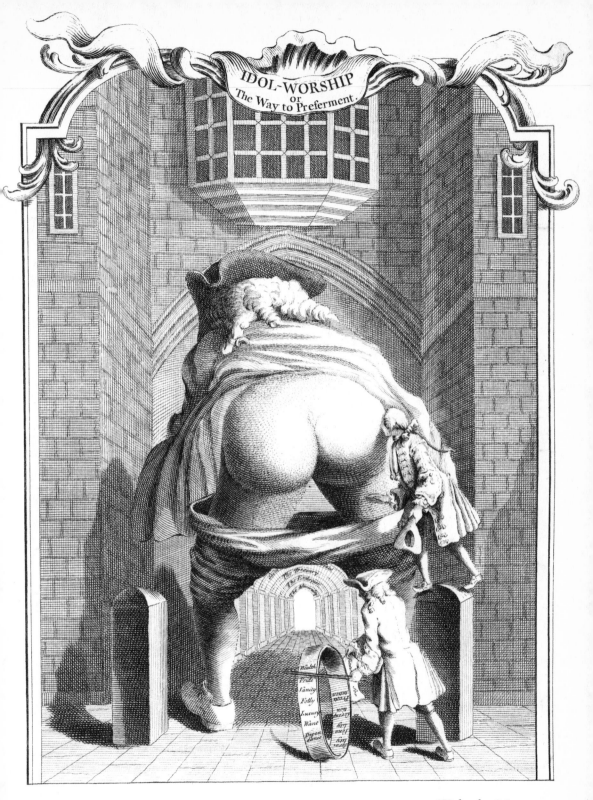

IDOL-WORSHIP
or
The Way to Preferment.

Walpole 25

Walpole also amassed a fortune, and was one of the few Prime Ministers to leave No. 10 much richer than when he entered. It was only in the 20th Century that Prime Ministers, following their departure from office, were able to make substantial sums from their memoirs and enjoy a golden retirement.

Walpole's huge wealth derived from the fact that the Government's balances at the end of each month were allowed to flow through his own

THE DEVIL UPON TWO STICKS, 1741

Walpole is carried across the mire of corruption by two MPs, so that none of the mud sticks to him. Other MPs are brushing the mud off their coats and Britannia weeps on the bank, while a canvasser picks her pocket for his bribes. This print, probably by Hubert Gravelot (1699–1773) was published in January 1741, on the eve of a General Election. The phrase, 'Every man has his price', was attributed, probably unfairly, to Walpole; but much of his success did come from the manipulation of Government jobs. Many went to his own family and relations – a process that was dubbed 'The Robinocracy'.

Walpole appointed his eldest son to the Rangership of Richmond Park because he wanted to have a lodge there for his own mistress. He turned it into a happy, second home. The key to his power was patronage, and in the notes which he meticulously made of his audiences with the King, over 90 per cent of the matters concerned jobs.

THE PATRIOT STATESMAN, 1740

Of the hundred or so cartoons that feature Walpole only two or three are favourable. It is quite likely that he commissioned them. This one, by Van der Gucht and published in 1740, was a reply to The English Colossus *and, selling for a shilling, it was widely circulated. It shows Burleigh, the great Elizabethan statesman, leading Walpole into the Temple of Fame to be welcomed by Minerva, the Goddess of Wisdom. Some of Walpole's critics had acquired the nickname of 'The Patriots'. This cartoon suggests that Walpole was turning the tables on them by claiming to be the true patriot. An early example of media manipulation!*

personal account, as First Lord of the Treasury, and he was able to invest the money. This practice ended with Walpole, but it allowed him to amass a vast personal fortune, to build a regal palace in Norfolk – Houghton Hall – and to assemble a superb collection of paintings. Sometimes he broke off a Cabinet meeting to look at a new painting. His collection, which was the finest made by any private person apart from the Royal Family, was sold after his death by his grandson to Catherine the Great of Russia, and it now forms the nucleus of the Hermitage Museum in St Petersburg. Walpole really was very rich. He spent £1, 219 3s 11d on the trimmings for his great State bed made for him by William Kent – the equivalent today would be in excess of £100,000. He relished the fruits of office and the trappings of power. He led a vigorous life with great gusto – hard-drinking, hunting, gargantuan meals with fine wine and, above all, intrigue.

THE LATE P-M-R M-N-R, 1743

*G*eorge Bickham was one of the first engravers to emerge as a leading political caricaturist in Britain. This print was published a year after Walpole's fall. The Tory, Jonathan Swift, who believed that Walpole the Whig had blocked his way to preferment in the Church, penned this verse about the man he loathed:

'And first, to make my observation
  right,
I place a statesman before my sight,
A bloated minister in all his geer,
With shameless visage, and perfidious
  leer;

Two rows of teeth arm each devouring
  jaw;
And, ostrich-like, his all-digesting
  maw,
My fancy drags this monster to my
  view
To shew the world his chief reverse in
  you.
Of loud unmeaning sounds a rapid
  flood
Rolls from his mouth in plenteous
  streams of mud;
With these the court and senate-house
  he plies,
Made up of noise, and impudence, and
  lies.'

28 Walpole

Walpole is called a Whig, but one should be wary about using party labels in the 18th Century. Political opinions held by Whig and Tory supporters blurred into each other. About the only fixed point in politics at that date was that all the Whigs could be regarded as supporters of the Hanoverian succession. So were some Tories, but others hankered for the Jacobites. Walpole's Government consisted of Whigs, as did other Governments down to the accession of George III in 1760. This did not mean that the Whigs invariably supported Walpole and towards the end of his supremacy some of them had become members of the Opposition.

In the early 1740s, the critics of Walpole began to get the upper hand. They were encouraged by the patriotic fervour in favour of the war with Spain. Even so, Walpole managed to survive a motion of censure which called for an inquiry into his conduct, and one of his major critics condemned him with the phrase 'Prime Minister' – 'an officer unknown to the law of Britain'. A few weeks later he was defeated on a minor matter in the House of Commons and relinquished his office. Thus the man who had played a vital part in building up the power of the House of Commons became the first head of an administration to be turned out of office by a vote in the House of Commons.

The cartoonists also wanted a distinctive feature by which Walpole could be recognized. They fixed upon the ribbon of the Garter. He even wore the blue ribbon when he was hunting, and he delighted in putting it across his Sunday best, which he wore to the House of Commons, and which the MPs resented. He was immensely proud of the fact that he was the first commoner to be made a Knight of the Garter for generations. So the cartoonists used the Garter as the badge of recognition for those who had never seen him; it was the visual expression of one of his nicknames, 'Sir Blue String'.

Walpole clearly did not like these cartoons, but the only action he took against them was occasionally to have the street sellers arrested and held for a few days. He thought that the pamphlets and the attacks on the stage, like John Gay's satirical *The Beggar's Opera* (1728), were much more damaging. The audience soon realized that MacHeath was meant to be Walpole, and the jolly wanton Polly Peachum was said to be Walpole's mistress, Maria Skerritt, who bore him two children and later became his wife. That led him to introduce censorship of the theatre; but he left prints alone, and we should all be grateful for that.

2 · The Pelhams

FIRST LORDS OF THE TREASURY

February 1742: Earl of Wilmington. *August 1743:* Henry Pelham
February 1746: Earl of Bath. *February 1746:* Henry Pelham
March 1754: 1st Duke of Newcastle
November 1756: 4th Duke of Devonshire. *June 1757:* Earl Waldegrave
June 1757–May 1762: 1st Duke of Newcastle

AFTER WALPOLE, there was no Colossus. George II was very pleased to appoint his former personal Treasurer, the Earl of Wilmington, as First Lord of the Treasury. Many years earlier, Wilmington – then known as Spencer Compton – had been a famous Speaker of the House of Commons. He was the leading Minister for 18 months, but was only a stop-gap, overshadowed by others, notably by the discontented Whig 'Patriot', Lord Carteret, and by Walpole's right-hand man in the House of Lords, the Duke of Newcastle. Horace Walpole, Robert's fourth son, said that his father was 'still minister behind the curtain'.

For most of the twenty years that followed Walpole's death in 1745, the political scene was dominated by the two brothers, Thomas Pelham Holles, the Duke of Newcastle, and Henry Pelham. Both held the office of First Lord of the Treasury and both had sufficient authority to entitle them to the dignity of being called Prime Minister.

The Pelhams used their immense wealth and power to manipulate patronage. After the defeat of the Jacobite Rebellion in 1745, George II

THE CONDUCT OF THE TWO BROTHERS, 1749

Britannia is disembowelled and quartered by Newcastle, wearing a ribbon inscribed 'Undertaker General', and his brother, Henry Pelham. Her amputated arms, Cape Breton and Gibraltar, refer to the territories that had recently been lost. Britannia's precious lifeblood flows into a pool labelled, 'Interest in our stocks, and national debt'. The pool is being lapped up by a white horse, a heraldic representation of the House of Hanover. Britannia's guts are being ripped out to feed the great army of hangers on and placemen. The poem attached to the print has the following couplet:

'A gripping vile degenerate Viper Brood,
That tears thy Vitals and exhausts thy Blood.'

Qui facit par alium, facit per se.

Quod factum est per alium, factum est per me.

Undertaker General

Gibraltar

Cape Breton

wanted to dispose of them. Horace Walpole, by no means an impartial observer, described Newcastle as 'a man of infinite intrigue without secrecy or policy and a Minister despised and hated by his master'. But the House of Commons and the City merchants threatened to cease funding the expensive European war – 'No Pelhams, No Money'. So the Pelhams returned, and were able to remain in office through adroit management of the Commons.

THE POLITICAL VOMIT FOR THE EASE OF BRITAIN, 1742

Wilmington was so obscure and politically insignificant that he appears in only two cartoons, and can scarcely be recognized in either. Here, wearing a tricorn hat, he kneels at the feet of Walpole and can only be distinguished by the fact that he is picking up the post of First Lord of the Treasury. Walpole has fallen. The political pygmies gather to grab the positions, offices and power that he is evacuating. The artist is D. Paulicino.

THE ANT CRAFTSMAN UNMASK'D, 1742

This depicts Pulteney, the Earl of Bath. He was a favourite of the press while he led the Opposition to Walpole and was associated with a periodical, The Craftsman, *which played an important part in undermining Walpole's authority. But when he became a serious contender for office, he too got it in the neck. The mask bearing the figure of Justice had been removed, showing Pulteney's face: the message of the cartoonist is that Pulteney was prepared to use the mask of an honest critic of a corrupt administration but in truth was no better himself. For a few days in 1746 he held the post of First Lord of the Treasury; he failed to survive because no one trusted him.*

A CHEAP AND EASY METHOD OF IMPROVING ENGLISH SWINE'S FLESH, 1744

*G*eorge II is shown as a swineherd, with all the leading politicians gorging themselves upon the fruits of office, which are depicted as pig ordure. Newcastle, recognizable from his glasses, tries to sweep up the mess, which is being created principally by his brother, Henry Pelham – the biggest pig on the right. This is the first time that a Prime Minister is shown as an animal. Pelham had just become Chancellor of the Exchequer, having surrendered his previous lucrative appointment as Paymaster of the Forces to the pig on his left. The print was a blunt and crude attack upon the endemic corruption of the Court and the Commons by the Pelham brothers.

Pelham said, 'The House of Commons is a great unwieldy body, which requires Art and some Cordial to keep it loyal; we have not many of the latter in our power.' But they had enough; and the cartoonists were very hard on them for the system of corrupt patronage over which they presided. In one cartoon they are depicted as pigs eating each other's droppings; Newcastle says, 'You eat it – damn 'em – there's nothing too nasty for them.' In another – surely one of the most savage cartoons of the 18th Century – they are seen disembowelling Britannia.

The Pelhams 33

THE COLE HEAVERS, 1756

Newcastle is depicted as an old fishwife dishing out the loot. Some goes to the Lord Chancellor, Hardwicke, because justice can be bought. More goes to Henry Fox, later Lord Holland, the most corrupt member of a corrupt government, described by a contemporary as 'the public defaulter of unaccounted millions'. He amassed a huge personal fortune which he left to his son, Charles James, who was to become much more famous than his father, whose fortune he managed to disperse. 'Cole' is slang for 'money' and it is also a play upon the old saying, 'Sending coals to Newcastle'.

The Government was very unpopular following the loss of Minorca by Admiral Byng. Newcastle, against the wishes of Pitt, insisted that Byng be tried and executed. This disgraceful event was memorably described by Voltaire as killing an Admiral 'pour encourager les autres'.

The Duke of Newcastle was a funny, fussy little man recognized by his large horn-rimmed glasses. He was the first Prime Minister to be depicted as a woman, in this case a fishwife. But, liking power and all that went with it, he hung on for as long as he could. He needed a strong Minister in the Commons and he appointed William Pitt the Elder, the future Earl of Chatham, who later came to dominate the Government. There were only two brief interruptions in the reign of the Pelhams. For a few days in 1746 the Earl of Bath was First Lord of the Treasury and for a short period from 1756 to 1757 first the Duke of Devonshire and then Earl Waldegrave held the office. Devonshire was dubbed 'the baby politician' by Horace Walpole. As for Waldegrave, there appears to be no surviving cartoon of him – surely the ultimate in obscurity. Newcastle returned in 1757, but in effect it was Pitt's Government.

PILLARS OF STATE, 1756

*T*his small drawing was reprinted
many times in the mid-18th
Century. On the left is Newcastle,
prissy as usual with his reading glasses.
On the right is the second Minister in
his Government – Henry Fox. They are
just about to lose office through their
casual conduct of the war against
France. The fleurs-de-lis in their
buttonholes indicate they had sold out
to the French at the beginning of the
Seven Years' War. The British ship-of-
state, supported by two gallows, is
upside down with a French cock
crowing on it.

The cartoon was probably by
George Townshend, who had been a
Colonel in the footguards. Later he
became a Marquis, the Irish Viceroy,
and a Field Marshal. He was a
colourful figure in the clubs and coffee
houses of London. Horace Walpole
said that these small cards 'are the
freshest treason; the portraits by
George Townshend are droll'.
Townshend was the only caricaturist
who was also a nobleman and a
leading politician.

ENTER WORTHIES, 1756

*T*he Duke of Devonshire is shown
kneeling before the King and
kissing hands on taking office. He was
so ineffectual that, although he was
First Lord of the Treasury for six
months, he did not feature in any other
cartoons.

3 · The Ascendancy of Chatham

FIRST LORDS OF THE TREASURY
May 1762: Earl of Bute. *April 1763:* George Grenville
July 1765: Marquis of Rockingham
August 1766–February 1770: Duke of Grafton
OFFICES HELD BY WILLIAM PITT, 1ST EARL OF CHATHAM
December 1756–April 1757: Secretary of State (Southern Department)
June 1757–October 1761: Secretary of State (Southern Department)
July 1766–November 1768: Lord Privy Seal (as Earl of Chatham)

AFTER the death of Henry Pelham in 1754, Britain had drifted into war with France – the Seven Years' War. The politician who dominated the scene was William Pitt the Elder, who later became Earl of Chatham. Pitt believed that the acquisition of an overseas empire was essential to develop and to expand trade. The merchants of the City of London were his greatest supporters and after his death they erected a noble monument to him in the Guildhall, praising his policy with the words, 'by commerce for the first time united with and made to flourish by war'. He was the first *de facto* Prime Minister to have a popular following in the country.

Pitt originally entered politics as a member of a young and rebellious group of Whigs, during the latter part of Walpole's 'reign'. For most of Pitt's career, however, it is difficult to find a suitable political label for him. It is also difficult to know whether he should really be called a Prime Minister, for he was never First Lord of the Treasury, but in practice he dominated successive governments, calling Cabinet meetings himself.

Pitt held the crucial position of Leader in the Commons when Newcastle was in the Lords. He was on bad terms with both the King and with Newcastle, but the dispute with Newcastle was patched up, while the King became grudgingly reconciled to the idea of Pitt playing a major part in the administration. Thus, in June 1757, a sort of diarchy was set up, with Newcastle as First Lord of the Treasury and Pitt as one of the two Secretaries of State: Newcastle attended to the political problems of the administration; Pitt concentrated on winning the war.

BRITANNIA'S GLORY, 1766

A very flattering portrayal of William Pitt on his elevation to the peerage as the Earl of Chatham. He carries the Staff of Maintenance and the Cap of Liberty, while Camden – his close friend and Lord Chancellor –

stands on the frustrated body of Envy. Minerva holds a laurel crown and Fame celebrates this joyous event. A fat and half-naked scribbler – one of those who dared to attack the Great Commoner for accepting a peerage – is whipped by the hangman.

To Pitt, the question of the war took precedence over all others, and he sought to unite everybody, whatever their political affiliations, in its support, saying, 'When trade is at stake you must defend it or perish.' In most cartoons of that period, Pitt is portrayed as a hero. From 1757 to 1761 he dominated the Newcastle administration. When it was rumoured that the King was going to remove him from office, 18 towns offered him their freedom. Dr Johnson said that Pitt was, 'a Minister given by the people to the king'. Pitt was instrumental in establishing British supremacy in India and Canada as the basis of the British Empire. The success of the British Navy was heralded in the song that was composed in 1759, 'Hearts of Oak'.

THE GHOST OF A D.....S TO W.....M P..T ESQ, 1746

In 1746 William Pitt, the scourge of the Government up to that time, took office under Henry Pelham as Vice-Treasurer of Ireland and very soon afterwards he became Paymaster General and a Privy Councillor. When Sarah, the famous Duchess of Marlborough, died in 1744 she bequeathed Pitt £10,000 – a sum that today would be in excess of £1 million – to continue his opposition to the Whigs and the 'German' policy of the King. She had wanted this to go on after her death, so when her hero joins the Government her ghost returns to claim the money back, and even the heavens respond with a great stroke of lightning.

SIC TRANSIT GLORIA MUNDI, 1762

*O*ne of the few prints of the early 1760s to attack Pitt, probably published by Bute's supporters. He is attacked for his vanity, pride, conceit and – strangely – for his patriotism, but not – and this is unusual in the 18th Century – for his venality. Indeed, one of the bubbles he has blown is 'Poverty' and therein is a two-fold criticism. First, the bubble attacks the high cost of waging the war, which the people had to bear, but secondly, it also emphasizes Pitt's own straitened circumstances, to which he drew attention in order to curry the favour of the mob. In 1761, when he left office, he reduced his household and advertised his carriage horses for sale. These actions were seen by his enemies as unnecessary, but were devilishly popular.

In 1760, when the war was still in full swing, George II suddenly died and was succeeded by his grandson, George III. The new King was a good deal less enthusiastic about Pitt than were the merchants and crowds of London. In October 1761, Pitt left office because he was unwilling to modify his pro-war policy.

For a time after Pitt's resignation, Newcastle remained First Lord of the Treasury, but the new King soon found a more congenial minister in the Earl of Bute, who had exerted considerable influence on George's education long before he came to the throne. It was widely believed, though probably untrue, that the King's widowed mother, the Princess of Wales, was Bute's mistress, and they were often coupled together in cartoons, some of which were obscene.

Bute was generally disliked by the English political classes – not least because he was a Scot. Many cartoons show him in a kilt and Scotch bonnet; and one shows him rubbing himself against a post in order to kill off lice. Bute's period in office lasted for less than a year. He was very unpopular, particularly after his attempt to impose a tax on cider. He was

THE JACK-BOOT EXALTED, 1762

A great many prints represent Bute as a Jack Boot – 'Jack Bute', since his first name was John. This engraving comments upon him being made a member of the Order of the Garter. He throws gold to the lean and hungry Scots, who are eager to share in the loot of office. The English Lion is in the shadows and the French Ambassador holds back the curtain. Bute wears a white favour in his bonnet, which implies Jacobite sympathies and therefore a tendency to betray his Protestant patron, George III. The figure on the extreme left is thought to be William Pitt, who is saying, 'I saw how it would be and retired in due time.' Pitt had resigned his office in October 1761 – six months before this print appeared.

'But ah the Whip is laid on those
Poor Southern Men he thinks his Foes
Who quickly give up their Places
To hungry Caledonian Faces.'

subjected to a sustained campaign through the media of the day and this was one of the factors that led him to give up office.

Cartoons hostile to Bute continued long after he ceased to be chief minister. Whenever anything went wrong, critics were disposed to blame it on Bute's influence over the King. Even after he left office the King continued to consult him. Today it would be taken for granted that the sovereign would only consult with serving ministers, not with other individuals whom he or she might prefer; but in the 18th Century this was not yet established constitutional practice.

THE ST-TE QUACK, 1762

*T*his is the most blatant attack upon Bute's supposed relationship with the Dowager Princess of Wales, the mother of George III. Bute is shown as a quack doctor carrying a clyster pipe with the words 'Union Squirt' on it. The woman lying on the tightrope is the Princess of Wales and she is being penetrated by a pole wearing a jackboot. The flag above them shows them embracing, with the proud boast: 'Performed here five times a day'. Among the quack's bottles is one labelled 'The Times', which refers to the print drawn by Hogarth that was favourable to Bute. In one corner a Scot and a Frenchman are re-affirming the 'auld alliance'.

The Ascendancy of Chatham 41

EXCISE – RESIGNATION, 1763

*T*he fall of Bute is celebrated in a double print. His Chancellor of the Exchequer had introduced a tax on cider and this, as in the case of Walpole, precipitated his downfall. It was so unpopular that Bute was physically assaulted and there were riots in the apple-growing areas of the West Country. There was the added twist that the Scots neither made nor drank cider. Within a month Bute resigned and he is shown here as hanging from an apple tree while a décoletée Princess of Wales weeps. To the right, the Devil tears Bute away by clutching at his private parts, with Bute plaintively pleading, 'Oh spare my manhood'.

THE STATE NURSERY, 1765

*A*n attack on Rockingham's administration, which lasted just a year. Rockingham is depicted as a small boy on a rocking horse, an allusion to his devotion to racing.

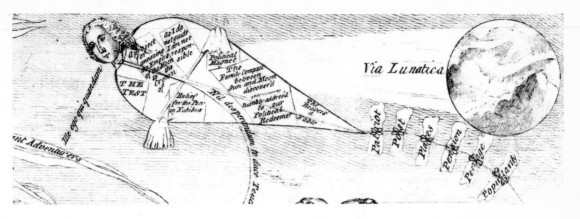

A POLITICAL FLIGHT TO THE MOON, 1766

Chatham is shown as a kite saying, 'A project for annexing the Empire of the Moon to the Crown'. Here is another attack upon Chatham's great imperial ambitions, but it is also a rare reference in a print to Chatham's mental instability. He suffered from *deep moods of depression bordering on insanity. The treatment for insanity at that time, as George III was to find, was crude. When Chatham was suffering from one of his relapses he had to live alone in a darkened room while his wife passed food to him through a hatch. His doctor was to father a future Prime Minister, Henry Addington (1801–04).*

After Bute, the reign of the Whig magnates resumed. His immediate successor as First Lord, George Grenville, fared even worse. The beginning of his administration coincided with the conclusion of the Seven Years' War, and critics were disposed to blame him for not pressing for an even more decisive victory. Horace Walpole was still more cutting: 'Scarce any man ever wore on his face such outward and visible marks of a hollow, cruel and rotten heart within.'

Grenville's biggest problem was the American colonies – the nucleus of the future United States. He had no wish to become embroiled in limitless wars with the native Americans in order to satisfy the land-hunger of the colonists, and sought to set the Mississippi as the western limit of expansion. Grenville incurred even more obloquy for an Act which his government introduced in 1765, requiring the British colonies in North America to pay for revenue stamps on certain goods. He was nicknamed 'The Stamper'. Following a huge outcry, the Government withdrew the stamps, which were held to be 'taxation without representation'. This episode was the first in a chain of events that led a decade later to the American War of Independence.

THE REPEAL, OR THE FUNERAL OF MISS AME-STAMP, 1766

*G*eorge Grenville was Chancellor of the Exchequer, as well as First Lord of the Treasury, from 1763 to 1765. On one occasion, during a Budget speech, he said that new taxes had to be raised, and he plaintively asked the House where he should raise them – repeating the question. Pitt mimicked him, using the words of the old song, 'Gentle Shepherd, tell me where'. That nickname stuck to him.

Grenville was also known as 'The Stamper' for introducing the tax on trade with the American colonies, the Stamp Act of 1765, which the colonies simply refused to pay. The refusal hit England's trade and the warehouses in this print are empty. Both the City and Chatham demanded that the Act should be repealed, as it duly was after less than a year.

The Repeal *was a very popular print and the publisher asserted that it was going to be published in spite of 'many Endeavours to prevent its Appearance'. He also identified a demand for it so great that it was 'beyond the Power of one workman to supply' all the copies required.*

Grenville's fall in 1765 was due more to his bad relations with the King than to the Stamp Act. Later in the decade, the rather shadowy figures of the Marquis of Rockingham and the Duke of Grafton occupied the post of First Lord of the Treasury successively. Grafton is depicted in cartoons with horns and a black cravat. The horns referred to his unhappy married life. He had divorced his wife – the only Prime Minister to do so – and openly kept as his mistress, Nancy Parsons, who was a courtesan.

THE BANDAGED CHATHAM, 1766

A simple etching made by a fellow MP, Mr Pryse Campbell, showing how handicapped Chatham had become – a food ravaged by gout and swathed in bandages, his arm in a sling, standing up in the House of Commons only with the aid of a crutch.

There was no great cartoonist in the period from 1750 to 1775 – when Pitt was the dominant political figure – so the prints are usually representational and crowded with figures. Chatham is recognized by his rather flat, long face, and gouty foot.

JANUS, 1768–69

The Duke of Grafton is here shown as 'Janus' facing both ways. But he also had two additional faces, looking upwards. The familiar tokens of recognition are present: the black cravat, and the horns of a cuckold. The print appeared in the periodical, the Political Register.

Grafton was renowned for his deviousness, and no one really knew what he stood for or what he was doing. This symbol of Janus could serve for several of his successors in the position of Prime Minister over the next two centuries.

THE POLITICAL WEDDING, 1769

In 1769, the Duke of Grafton had been divorced from his first wife, on the grounds of her adultery. He openly kept a mistress, Nancy Parsons, who lived above a perfumery shop in Soho. She is shown weeping in this cartoon, but her grief was lessened by a pension of £300 per annum – a large sum in those days. Grafton is shown marrying a Miss Wrottesley, a niece of the Duchess of Bedford, to find some respectability. The author of the 'Junius letters' poured vitriol upon the Duke of Grafton; four days after this cartoon appeared, he wrote: 'Marriage is the point on which a rake is stationary at last; and truly, my Lord,

you may well be weary of the circuit you have taken, for you have now fairly travelled through every sign in the political zodiac, from the Scorpion in which you stung Lord Chatham, to the hopes of a Virgin in the House of Bloomsbury.'

Grafton experienced what no other Prime Minister has by the combination of being cuckolded by his wife, divorcing her, keeping a mistress, and then abandoning the latter to marry a younger woman.

This print appeared in the periodical, the Oxford Magazine, which survived as a magazine of topical comment for about five years.

In 1766 Pitt (who had by then become Earl of Chatham) returned to exert the dominant influence. This time, he occupied the post of Lord Privy Seal. His health was poor, and his sanity dubious. After a strange period of a couple of years in which everyone found it extremely difficult to transact any business with the principal member of the Government, Chatham resigned.

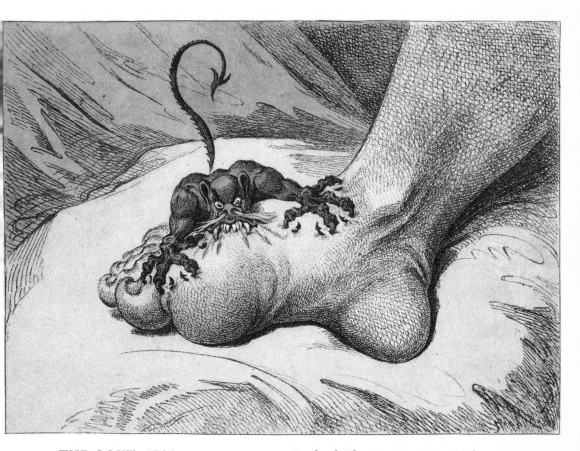

THE GOUT, 1799

Gout, celebrated here by Gillray, was one of the great afflictions of the 18th Century. It was aggravated by the excessive drinking of port, which was very cheap as a result of the Treaty of Oporto (1704), cementing the friendship between Portugal and England. There were no cures, only oils, ointments and bandages to swathe the agony. Elegant stools were made as footrests. Gout affected only the extremities and did not attack the vital organs. Many politicians, notably Chatham, suffered intensely, but even 19th-Century politicians, like Disraeli, also suffered from it.

The Ascendancy of Chatham 47

4 · Lord North and After

FIRST LORDS OF THE TREASURY
February 1770: Lord North (later 2nd Earl of Guilford)
March 1782: Marquis of Rockingham (2nd administration)
July 1782: 2nd Earl of Shelburne (later 1st Marquis of Lansdowne)
April 1783–December 1783: 3rd Duke of Portland

IN 1770 the King at last found a head of government with whom he was able to work for a long period: Lord North, who had been Chancellor of the Exchequer under Grafton. North, like Lord Bute before him and the younger Pitt after him, is sometimes called a 'Tory'; but in all three cases the name signifies in practice 'a minister particularly acceptable to George III'.

Lord North had many endearing qualities. Unlike most of his predecessors, he had a sense of humour and an easy-going temper. Horace Walpole said of him: 'Though his country was ruined under his administration he preserved his good humour.' He was a skilled parliamentarian and a man of high moral character. He is the first Prime Minister who is easily recognizable in the cartoons – short, plump, a long sloping forehead and an ample double chin. The early cartoons from the 1700s are generally favourable, and – like Walpole – he was depicted as a parliamentary juggler. But the later ones are sharply critical and show him as a vacillator, humiliated over the loss of the American colonies. On several occasions he asked George III to relieve him of his responsibilities, though the King – drawing upon his personal loyalty – persuaded him to stay.

It was North's misfortune to be in office when Britain lost her colonies in America. In the decades preceding his Ministry, the colonies had become increasingly conscious of their own power and importance, and resented the imposition of taxes, especially the Stamp Duty. They won the sympathy and eloquent support of such significant politicians as Chatham and Edmund Burke. Chatham spoke of reconciliation, saying: 'The colonies were too great an object to be grasped but in the arms of affection.'

The Colossus of the North; or The Striding Boreas.

See our Colossus strides with Trophies crownd:
And Monsters in Corruption's Stream abound

THE COLOSSUS OF THE NORTH, 1774

North held elections in 1774 and kept his majority. This print echoes a similar one about Walpole. Both Prime Ministers are shown to be giants among pygmies. North straddles the River of Corruption, which flows out from Westminster Hall, carrying MPs whose re-election North had secured. He has papers in his hand marked Places, Pensions and Lottery Tickets. Lottery tickets were frequently given as bribes; on one occasion, George II asked Walpole to buy a bundle of lottery tickets for one of his mistresses.

49

THE ABLE DOCTOR, OR AMERICA SWALLOWING THE BITTER DRAUGHT, 1774

As a punishment for the Boston Tea Party, which took place in 1773, North introduced a Bill to close the Port of Boston and to bring the recalcitrant colony to heel. Britannia weeps as Bute wields a sword engraved with 'Military Laws'. Mansfield, the Lord Chief Justice, holds down America, as North pours tea down her throat, which she spits back at him. Within a year of this cartoon, fighting had broken out in North America. North responded with another Bill to prohibit all trade with America and to allow the seizure of ships.

The prints in these years were overwhelmingly critical of North's and Bute's policies in America.

The dramatic incident that started the chain of events leading to Independence was the Boston Tea Party of 1773. Tea consumed in North America came from India and was transported in vessels operated by the British-owned East India Company. For a long time that trade had been conducted through Britain and the tea was subject to a heavy duty. The latter was deeply resented in North America and was largely circumvented by a very active smuggling industry.

Then the British Government decided to permit tea to pass directly from India to America, and simultaneously made a great reduction in the duty. This action might have been expected to produce a large increase in tea consumption in North America, with tea smuggling becoming unprofitable. In fact, North's decision angered both the smugglers and the American patriots, who believed they should be making taxation decisions for themselves.

THE PRIVY COUNCIL, 1780

*N*orth had been in office for ten years and the cartoonists were becoming much harder on him. Here he presides over a Privy Council meeting at a boghouse. He is using as lavatory paper the proposals from the counties to reduce corruption and to reform the Government. One of the accusations was that North was using state money to improve his own house in Bushy Park.

LORD NORTH IN THE SUDS, 1782

*T*his refers to the crisis that led to North's fall. He increased the duty on soap for the first time in 66 years, as well as those on salt and tobacco. As everyone used salt and most used

soap, these taxes were very unpopular. North is being assaulted by fishwives, laundresses and working women, one of whom is also smoking. Charles James Fox snarls, but within a year he was to form with North one of the strangest coalitions in British history. The artist is T. Colley.

Oh do but look how black his Arse is

To BROOKS'S

To be Lett:
either as a Gibbet
or Direction Post.

THE KETTLE HOOTING THE PORRIDGE POT, 1782

*O**n Rockingham's death, Shelburne was appointed First Lord of the Treasury. Fox resigned, since he could not stand Shelburne, and he is shown running off to his gambling cronies at*

Brooks's Club. Shelburne was disliked by the cartoonists. Although he was thought to be the cleverest man in Britain, he was called 'The Jesuit' and sometimes 'Malagrida' after a notorious Portuguese priest. Here Gillray produced one of the most obscene cartoons of the 18th Century.

A group of colonists disguised as American Indians threw the imported tea into Boston harbour. In response, the British closed the port of Boston and suspended the charter of the colony of Massachusetts, in the hope that other North American ports and colonies would welcome the diverted trade and side with the British Government in the quarrel. But this did not happen. The cartoonists seized upon the episode and depicted North as forcing tea down America's throat. He had become a figure of fun.

In 1774, a meeting of the American Congress was convened, with representatives from the various colonies. In April 1775, the first engagement between the colonials and British military forces took place at Lexington. In July 1776 came the formal American Declaration of

Independence. In the long war that followed, the British Army was defeated and had to surrender ignominiously. After the surrender of Yorktown in 1781, North could take no more; early in 1782 he resigned.

North's successor as First Lord of the Treasury was the Marquis of Rockingham, who returned to office after an absence of more than fifteen years, but was to die a few months later. There are not many cartoons of him. He was succeeded by the Earl of Shelburne, who had no substantial support in Parliament.

Shelburne is easily recognized in the cartoons – swarthy, sly and with a compliant, devious smile. When he had difficulty in concluding the peace negotiations with America, North and Charles James Fox, from two different political poles, united to bring him down in 1783. This was an unholy alliance and the cartoonists loved it. The Fox-North coalition only lasted a year, but it is one of the most cartooned events in the 18th

CARLO KHAN'S TRIUMPHAL ENTRY INTO LEADENHALL STREET, 1783

Carlo Khan's triumphal Entry into Leadenhall Street.

The most famous cartoon of the coalition. Fox had introduced a measure to transfer control of the patronage of the East India Company to the Government. He is clearly the leading figure in the coalition, for he is sitting on the elephantine North, who is himself being led by Edmund Burke, the great publicist for this odd couple, through Leadenhall Street to the India Office. On the flag beside him, 'Man of the People' is struck out and replaced by 'King of Kings'.

Fox believed that this cartoon did him more damage than any speech in Parliament. It was drawn by James Sayers, who was trained as a lawyer. On coming to London in 1780, he started to draw and continued to do so for about fifteen years. His cartoons are rather flat and darkly etched, but in the 1780s his work was as widely known as Gillray's. He was violently opposed to Fox and later Pitt gave him a pensioned sinecure.

THE COALITION DISSECTED, 1783

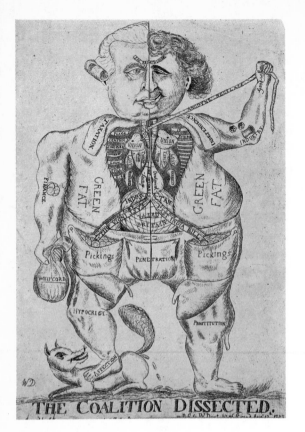

THE COALITION DISSECTED.

*T*he Fox-North coalition was one of the most cartooned events of the 18th Century. The cartoonists gloried in the disparity between the Tory North and the Whig Fox. In this joint portrait, the word 'Truth' is reversed on their tongues, for both got the pickings from the East India Bill, and Fox's many weaknesses are emphasized. There were many jokes about Fox's sexual activities; in this cartoon, 'Prostitution' is written on his leg, while on the front of his breeches 'Penetration' is proclaimed. Fox's love of gambling is shown by the dice-box and dice on his arm, which are labelled 'Industry'.

The artist is William Dent, who was active from 1783 to 1793. His cartoons are naive but vivid, direct and lewd; their crude vigour made them very popular.

Century. North was depicted as an old woman and Fox as a drunken reprobate; chamber pots were emptied over North's head, while Court officials offered Fox the daintiest dishes. The veneer of respectability of this extraordinary alliance was offered by the Duke of Portland, the nominal Prime Minister, who is usually portrayed as a grey and shadowy figure.

Before 1783, Parliament had destroyed ministries that the King favoured; but this was the first time that the King was actually compelled to accept a ministry, which he found profoundly distasteful, because Parliament forced it upon him.

The coalition did ratify the peace treaty with the former American colonies, but it was brought down over proposals to reform the East India Company. The cartoonists were in no doubt that the main purpose was to transfer the vast patronage of the East India Company into the pockets of Fox and the coalition. In one particularly famous cartoon Fox is depicted as clearly in charge of the heavy, ponderous, elephantine North.

The Beast that thou sawest, WAS and IS NOT, and shall ascend out of the Bottomless Pitt, and go into Perdition, and they that dwell on the Earth shall wonder when they behold the Beast that WAS, and IS NOT, and yet IS.
Rev.C17.V8.

Coalition

Pub. April 2d 1783 by W.Humphrey No 227 Strand near Temple Bar.

THE MONSTER, 1783

This cartoon came out on the day that the new coalition Government was formed. The head of the monster is Portland, the nominal Prime Minister, but the two buttocks are North and Fox. The poem beneath reads:

'The Head is Portland with the tail a Fox,
Each different mouth bawls loudly for itself,
Yet all agree in one thing, Snack the Pelf.'

The cartoon is ascribed to J. Boyne, a former actor who turned to drawing and who also produced many social satires.

Lord North and after 55

JUNCTION OF PARTIES, 1783

The Devil stirs the chamber pot into which North and Fox are defecating. Many prints of the late 18th Century are concerned with bodily functions – spitting, farting, defecating and urinating. They were designed to shock and to remind everybody that the veneer of civilization on the Court and on politicians was pretty thin. Cartoonists preferred scatology to sexual obscenity.

THE PARODY – OR MOTHER COLE AND LOADER, 1784

North is depicted as the sanctimonious bawd, Mother Cole, and Fox as the sharping gamester from a popular play by Foote. The words of the play are cleverly parodied in North's comments, 'Eighteen years I have paid Scott and Lot – and during the whole time nobody have said Mrs North why do you so? Unless twice that I was threatened with impeachment and three times with a Halter!' The irony lies in the fact that Fox is a new-found friend, for it was he who had earlier threatened North with impeachment.

This was one of a series of cartoons drawn by Thomas Rowlandson of the Fox-North coalition and the famous Westminster election of 1784. Rowlandson's gifts are best seen in his paintings and drawings of the social life of the late 18th Century. His political cartoons have a much softer line and comment than those of Gillray.

The Government's proposals passed the Commons. The King personally disliked Charles James Fox, who, he believed, was leading his son, the Prince of Wales, astray. Then the King made it plain that any peer supporting the proposals would be counted as a personal enemy. The Lords took the message and threw out the Bill, and the King dismissed the Portland administration.

Lord North and after 57

5 · The Era of Pitt

FIRST LORDS OF THE TREASURY
December 1783: William Pitt the Younger
February 1801: Henry Addington (later 1st Viscount Sidmouth)
May 1804–January 1806: William Pitt the Younger

THE KING was only able to take the dramatic action of dismissing the coalition because he had at last found a man on whom he could rely: William Pitt the Younger, second son of the Earl of Chatham. The new First Lord of the Treasury was an astounding political phenomenon. In 1783 he was only twenty-four years of age, but he had already served as Chancellor of the Exchequer under Shelburne. He had politics on both sides of his family, for his mother was the sister of George Grenville. Pitt soon established a primacy over his colleagues. There was no doubt that he really was the Prime Minister; and most of his successors were the effective leaders of the Government and the country.

Pitt's administration coincided with the Golden Age of English caricature. It was dominated by James Gillray (1756–1815), who started drawing in the early 1780s and was still working nearly 30 years later. He is the greatest English caricaturist, but he counted among his contemporaries Rowlandson, Sayers, Newton and Dent. They cut their drawings with a steel knife onto a copper plate and ink was poured into these fine incisions to create the lines of the print.

The cartoonists worked at a frantic rate, for the prints were needed as comments upon the political events of the day. The cartoons' sale depended upon their promptness and relevance. They were displayed in the windows of print shops, to be sold to the passing public at about 6d plain or 1 shilling coloured. Politics was no longer the preserve of the

THE MONSTROUS HYDRA, OR VIRTUE INVULNERABLE, 1789

A flattering image, which shows Pitt during the Regency crisis, when the Opposition thought that they would take over since the Prince of Wales would become Regent. The *Hydra of Pandemonium is crowned by the Prince of Wales's feathers and all the various heads are Pitt's opponents – North being blindfolded. The Sun of Public Good breaks through the clouds of North's 'Debts and Deficiencies', which had arisen from the American wars, and shines down upon the virtuous head of William Pitt.*

THE POLITICAL CONTEST, 1787

F ox and Pitt were one of the great double acts in cartooning history. Here, for a change, Fox is winning. He had opposed the Shop Tax, introduced in 1785 and levied upon rent. It was most unpopular in London and in 1787 Pitt had to reduce it; two years later, he withdrew the tax altogether. In this cartoon, everyone is fighting – Sheridan sits on the Lord Chancellor's back; Burke has Warren Hastings by the collar; and Lord North is throttling John Wilkes.

political elite. The middle classes, and even those who could not write, could see the pictorial representations of the follies of the leading politicians. There were several print shops in central London, vying with each other to capture the latest political events. Gillray was principally employed by Hannah Humphrey, the owner of such a shop in Bond Street. He was so close to her that he actually took lodgings there, and was to die in his room above the shop.

Pitt was defeated in the House of Commons several times during the first few months of his premiership, but these defeats were not considered to be resigning matters. In March 1784, when he was defeated by one vote, he decided he was strong enough to chance an election. Like James Callaghan just under 200 years later, he took defeat by a single vote as an occasion for calling a General Election. The results were very different. In the General Election of 1784 there was, for the first time, a clear Government leader, Pitt, and a clear Opposition leader, Charles James Fox. Rivalry between these two dominated the following twenty years of British politics.

In the early years Pitt was depicted as a young hero, though not for long. In 1789 his tenure of office was threatened when George III became temporarily insane and a Regency seemed likely. Fox was a crony of the Prince of Wales and it looked as if his chance had come. Pitt was saved by the King regaining his sanity, but during this Regency crisis, the Prime Minister was depicted as the enemy of the Constitution.

Unlike many 18th-Century politicians, Pitt was not personally corrupt. The only sinecure he held was that of Lord Warden of the Cinque Ports. He was to die with heavy debts, which Parliament willingly paid. Yet the system over which he presided was corrupt, and in one cartoon he was shown as a toadstool flourishing on the dung-heap of patronage.

Pitt is invariably drawn as a very thin figure – the bottomless pit; the darning needle. Cartoonists knew two things about him – he drank a lot and he seemed to have no interest in the ladies. Indeed, the wits said that Pitt was stiff with everyone except the ladies. He is drawn with a flushed and mottled face; Gillray depicted him visibly drunk.

Pitt had no inclination for romantic affairs. A famous cartoon of him making advances to the Bank of England, the 'Old Lady of Threadneedle

THE GIANT FACTOTUM AMUSING HIMSELF, 1797

In one of the most famous images of Pitt, he straddles Parliament, crushing the opposition with one foot, while the other is supported by his cronies. He plays with the world and money falls from his pockets. This etching by Gillray marks the emergence of the Prime Minister as a national hero, following in his father's footsteps. It was used by Canning as the frontispiece for The Anti-Jacobin, *a political magazine which attacked radical politicians.*

The Era of Pitt 61

AN EXCRESCENCE – A FUNGUS ALIAS A TOADSTOOL UPON A DUNGHILL, 1791

Gillray produced this cartoon before he accepted a pension from the Government. It portrays the corrupt system of royal patronage that Pitt had to use, seemingly willingly.

THE POLITICAL LOCUST, 1795

In 1795, there was a great deal of unrest. Food prices were high; new taxes on hair powder and insurance were introduced to pay for the war with France. Pitt's house in Downing Street was besieged by a mob. Here he is attacked for making his brother the Lord Privy Seal, for removing constitutional liberties and for resisting sensible parliamentary reform. This cartoon was by Isaac Cruikshank, a prolific and uneven cartoonist.

GOD SAVE THE KING, 1795

Pitt and his bosom friend, Dundas, are carousing – they have emptied one brandy decanter and five bottles of wine. They are both 'tired and emotional', and a chamber pot stands ready. There were several prints at this time that depicted Pitt the worse for drink. Two years later, Canning offered a pension to Gillray and the drunkenness disappeared.

WILLIAM THE CONQUEROR'S TRIUMPHAL ENTRY!!!, 1795

*W*ith the threat of invasion, Pitt proposed to increase the militia by 60,000, which was condemned by Fox 'as a measure for impressing the subjects of this country'. Pitt decided to finance the militia by a 'Loyalty Loan' of £18 million, but he told the bankers in the City that if it was undersubscribed then he would increase taxes. The result was a triumph, for it was completely subscribed in 5 days. The Duke of Bridgewater handed in a single draft at sight for £100,000. In Richard Newton's cartoon, Dundas leads Pitt into the Treasury, while Fox and other alleged Jacobins scowl in anger.

Newton also produced some very funny cartoons of the royal family. He was a master of the grotesque, whose talents were lost too soon when he died at the age of 21.

WILLIAM the CONQUEROR'S TRIUMPHAL ENTRY!!!

Street', was funny because everyone knew that making advances to ladies was just what Pitt was hopeless at. Gillray did, however, produce a very flattering cartoon of Pitt as the Giant Factotum, dominating the Commons and playing with the world. However, he contrived to place the Coat of Arms of the Speaker's Chair right in the centre of Pitt's groin.

At this time George Canning, a young and gifted supporter of Pitt and a future Prime Minister, was the editor of a magazine, *The Anti-Jacobin*, which attacked the revolutionary fervour sweeping France and threatening Britain. Canning also approached Gillray in 1797 and gave him money to draw more flattering cartoons of Pitt. Gillray's etching needle was bought. Canning wanted to appear himself in a cartoon, and asked Gillray to include him. He did this in a cartoon showing the horrors of the French Revolution, in which Fox flogs Pitt, and Canning is shown hanging on a lamp post. To be caricatured was to be recognized.

Pitt had to deal with the consequences of the French Revolution. Above all, the English monarchy had to be protected and he was shown frequently as the defender of George III. He introduced repressive mea-

The Era of Pitt 63

THE DEVIL'S DARNING NEEDLE, 1795

*R*ichard Newton's caricature emphasizes the 'bottomless Pitt', its style more characteristic of the mid-19th Century than the late 18th.

BILLY'S POLITICAL PLAYTHING, 1796

A graphic image of the Pitt/Fox rivalry by Richard Newton.

sures, including the suspension of Habeas Corpus – the right to resist imprisonment without trial – to prevent revolutionary ideas taking a grip in Britain. This resulted in his critics depicting him as a locust feeding off the Constitution, and – absurdly – as someone who even had aspirations to the Crown for himself.

In order to finance the war with France, Pitt introduced Income Tax in 1799, and a spate of cartoons shows him placing a great burden upon the shoulders of John Bull. He was not a great war leader like his father, but he patiently cobbled together a series of alliances to contain Napoleon. This earned him the flattery of Gillray in the famous cartoon of Pitt and Napoleon carving up the world as if it were a large plum pudding. Later cartoonists have frequently parodied the cartoon in a contemporary setting.

The greatest double act in cartoon history was Pitt and Fox. They were complete contrasts. Fox was fat, indulgent, a gambler, a womaniser and a spendthrift. He created the role of Leader of the Opposition by speaking off the cuff in the House of Commons with compelling oratory. He always attacked the Government, even when it was engaged in fighting Napoleon, and so he is shown repeatedly as a friend of the revolutionaries with blood on his hands. Fox is also drawn without a wig and wearing ordinary town clothes, which emphasizes his position as a man of the people. He was not smart, but rather down at heel, appealing to the 'working class'.

Pitt fell from office in 1801 because of Ireland. In 1798 nationalist ideas sparked off by the French Revolution set off an insurrection in Ireland. That country in the late 18th Century had a Parliament of its own, which was composed of Protestant landowners in an overwhelmingly Catholic and peasant society, but it was an Irish Parliament nevertheless. The insurrection involved much wanton brutality on both sides, but in the end it was suppressed. Pitt's reaction was to opt for the political and economic union of Britain and Ireland. This entailed suppressing the Irish Parliament and giving Irish MPs seats at Westminster. By wholesale bribery, Pitt's Government persuaded the Parliament at Dublin to commit suicide: the 'Union' was established.

As part of an Irish 'package deal' Pitt, recognizing that the Catholics had to be reconciled to the Union, proposed to remove the legal barriers against Catholic MPs sitting in the House of Commons. George III simply would not accept this, for he regarded 'Catholic emancipation' as contrary to his Coronation Oath. Neither Pitt nor the King would give way and in February 1801 Pitt left office.

MIDAS TRANSMUTTING ALL INTO PAPER, 1797

In February 1797, there was a run on the Bank of England and a drain on gold. Pitt stopped the Bank issuing gold. Notes in denominations of £1 and £2 were introduced. These supplemented the existing £5 and £10 notes, which were only used by a very small number of people in London. Pitt was strongly attacked by Fox for the measure.

Gillray's cartoon depicts Pitt in a rather ambiguous light. He is the Colossus controlling the money supply, spewing out pound notes, but peeping through the crown of notes on his head are the ears of an ass.

LILLIPUTIAN-SUBSTITUTES, EQUIPPING FOR PUBLIC SERVICE, 1801

*T*he incoming Government of Addington was seen to be an administration of pygmies. Addington is lost in Pitt's jack-boot, coat and hat. Some days before this cartoon appeared, Fox had said: 'the King may not rule us only by his Jack-boot, but we may be governed by his Jack-boots' Jack-boot'. Hawkesbury, later to be Prime Minister as Lord Liverpool, is lost in a pair of large trousers; the obscure Hobart is lost in Dundas's kilt; another obscurity cannot fill Canning's slippers. It is always difficult to follow a Colossus like Pitt, but Gillray's cartoon is not an unfair comment on the inadequacy of his successors.

INTEGRITY RETIRING FROM OFFICE, 1801

*T*here were suggestions that Pitt resigned in 1801 because he did not want to make peace with France, but Gillray explicitly attributes the resignation to Ireland. Pitt holds in his hand a paper which says 'Justice of Emancipating Catholicks'. He is followed by his oldest political friend, Dundas, and his Foreign Secretary, Grenville. Pitt was recalled three years later.

THE PLUMB PUDDING IN DANGER – STATE EPICURES TAKING UN PETIT SOUPER, 1805

*B*ritain, alone of the European nations, had remained unconquered by France. The two political giants are dividing up the world. Pitt gets the West Indies and Napoleon gets Holland, Spain and Italy, but, notably, not Russia or Sweden. This famous cartoon was one of the last that Gillray drew of Pitt, who died a few months later.

The King then appointed Henry Addington, the Speaker of the House of Commons, as Prime Minister. For the second time, the long ministry of a man with exceptional abilities was followed by the much briefer ministry of a little man. As a contemporary jingle put it:

> *As London is to Paddington*
> *So is Pitt to Addington*

Addington was one of the most inconsequential of Prime Ministers and had a hard time at the hands of the cartoonists. His father was a doctor, not a member of the landed nobility, and he was never allowed to forget his humble origins. He was sometimes drawn carrying a clyster pipe, the instrument used by doctors to give an enema – something of a cure-all in the medicine of the day. In other cartoons he carries a bottle of medicine, a box of pills, or a doctor's bag.

In March 1802, Addington and the French attempted a sort of settlement – the Peace of Amiens. But neither side trusted the other and in little over a year Britain declared war on France. The clamour started for Pitt to come back and he did in 1804. In October 1805 the British won the great sea victory at Trafalgar, but two months later the allies were crushed by the defeat of the Russians and Austrians at Austerlitz, the Battle of the Nations, and the alliance which Pitt had put together was shattered.

Pitt, at 46 years of age, was worn out. In January 1806 the burden of being Prime Minister for nineteen years, and his predilection for port, finally killed him.

6 · War and Reaction

FIRST LORDS OF THE TREASURY

January 1806: Lord Grenville ('Ministry of All the Talents')
March 1807: 3rd Duke of Portland. *September 1809:* Spencer Perceval
June 1812–February 1827: 2nd Earl of Liverpool

THERE was no obvious successor to Pitt, although Gillray in a rather later cartoon showed Pitt's mantle prematurely falling on to Canning. The King turned to Lord Grenville, the son of one of his previous Prime Ministers, George Grenville. As he drew upon the range of politicians from the right to the left, the Government was dubbed, ironically, the 'Ministry of All the Talents'. Fox, whose health was failing, was made Foreign Secretary – his first post for twenty years. He found that making peace with France on acceptable terms was impossible and his death soon afterwards weakened an already rickety Government.

The Government was also dubbed the 'Broad-Bottomed Ministry', which described both its political character and the physical attributes of some of its members. Gillray produced a series of very funny cartoons focusing upon the bottoms. The only important act to the Government's credit was the abolition of the slave trade, but existing slaves in British colonies were not freed for another twenty-five years.

After just over a year in office, the 'Broad Bottoms' were driven out on the same issue that had defeated Pitt in 1801 – relief for Roman

THE PIGS POSSESSED – OR THE BRAVE POLITICAL LITTER RUNNING HEADLONG INTO THE SEA OF . . . ., 1807

George III was not prepared to accept the relatively mild measure of Catholic emancipation proposed by Lord Grenville and the 'Ministry of All the Talents', so he forced the Government to resign. In a cartoon reminiscent of the story of the Gadarene swine, Gillray depicts him in one of the popular guises, 'Farmer George', pushing the ungrateful grunters over the cliff. Grenville and Howick, later Earl Grey of the 1832 Reform Act, are the first to hit the water. The one who is most reluctant to leave and who is still on the cliff is Sheridan, the politician and playwright. He is recognizable here with his harlequin's clothes and drinker's nose. Having waited over thirty years for office, Sheridan was most reluctant to leave and to surrender his Seals.

A KEEN SIGHTED POLITICIAN WARMING HIS IMAGINATION, 1795

Ten years before Grenville became Prime Minister, Gillray had already decided to focus upon his broad bottom.

Catholics. Grenville proposed that Catholics should be allowed to hold army commissions – hardly a revolutionary proposal at a time when Britain was giving eager support to foreign Catholic monarchs. This was too much for George III, who forced him to resign. The episode was portrayed by Gillray as Farmer George driving the pigs over the cliff. Like many cartoons of the late 18th and early 19th Centuries, it casts light on the deep anti-Catholic feeling of the time.

The King turned to another politician, the Duke of Portland, who had presided over the Fox-North coalition of 1783. In ill-health and virtually senile, Portland was often not told of Cabinet meetings. Portrayed as a grey figure in Portland stone, he was overshadowed by his two leading Ministers – Canning and Castlereagh – who disliked each other so much that they fought a duel.

After 18 months, Portland was replaced by Spencer Perceval, who was a successful lawyer but a plodder. Perceval had 'strong and invincible prejudices on many subjects', and in particular upon Catholicism, which he was determined to keep in a subordinate place in Britain. As Canning and Castlereagh refused to serve, his was a third-rate administration. Perceval had a cold and ungenial nature; he is portrayed in cartoons wearing lawyer's clothes and as a fussy, bald little man who lived up to his nickname, 'Little P'. On 12 May 1812, as he entered the House of Commons, Perceval was shot by a madman, Henry Bellingham. He was the only Prime Minister to be assassinated, and for this he is remembered. Bellingham was tried and executed within a week; and the House of Commons voted Perceval's widow £50,000, which is roughly equivalent to £2 million today. Grief, however, was not universal. The Luddite riots by bands of workers resisting mechanization had broken out in 1812 and Perceval had shown no understanding of how to deal with them. His death was said to have been greeted in the Potteries by a crowd running down the street shouting, 'Perceval is shot, Hurrah!'.

By this time, George III was considered to be permanently insane and so it was the Regent, later to be George IV, who appointed Lord Liverpool to be the next Prime Minister. He was to hold the office for 15 years, longer than anyone except Walpole. He presided over some very dramatic events – the victory at Waterloo, the depression after the Napoleonic Wars, the Luddite riots, the Peterloo Massacre, and the Cato Street Conspiracy, whose purpose was the assassination of all the Cabinet. Liverpool's calm resolve saw Britain through a true crisis that followed the French wars and ensured that Britain did not succumb to a revolution.

Although Liverpool was only out of office for thirteen months in the period from 1793 until his health broke down in 1827, he was never really seen as a dominating leader. He believed all ministers to be equal and he never actually dismissed one of his own. His modest attitude is rather surprising: before being Prime Minister he had been War Secretary, Home Secretary and Foreign Secretary, and six of the next ten Prime Ministers served in his Cabinet.

JOHN BULL
CONTEMPLATING A STATUE
OF THE PORTLAND STONE,
1807

After the collapse of the 'Ministry of All the Talents' on the question of Catholic commissions, the Duke of Portland formed his second administration. He was deaf, gouty and infirm – a mere figurehead. As far as the King was concerned, his outstanding merit was that he was not going to stir things up over Catholic emancipation. The artist is Charles Williams.

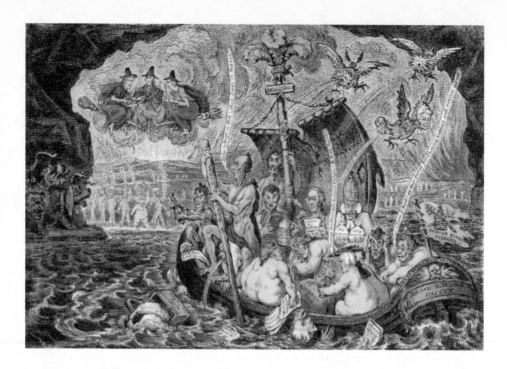

CHARON'S BOAT – OR – THE GHOSTS OF 'ALL THE TALENTS' TAKING THEIR LAST VOYAGE, 1807

This is Gillray depicting the leaky, sinking boat of the 'Broad-Bottomed Ministry', with its ragged and broken sail, 'Catholic Emancipation'. It is drifting towards Hell, where Fox and Cromwell welcome it. The tall figure holding the pole is Howick, who is quoting from Milton's Paradise Lost, *'Better to reign in Hell than serve in Heaven'. Grenville is the fat bottom on the right with the chalice and the Cardinal's hat. Next to him are two other members of the Government, both Grenvilles, one of whom is losing his sinecures overboard. Sheridan vomits. The game was up for this Government, which was always fairly chaotic. Grenville simply could not hold them together any longer and cope with the King's rejection of Catholic emancipation.*

In the cartoons, Liverpool is a shadowy figure, usually to one side or in the background, but recognizable through his extraordinary profile, which is like a walnut. Disraeli, at a later date, called him 'The Arch Mediocrity'. Yet it is difficult to believe that a man could remain Prime Minister for nearly fifteen consecutive years without some qualities other than tenacity. Even during the crisis of 1819, Liverpool was not a hate figure for the cartoonists or the pamphleteers. They fired at his ministers, Castlereagh, Addington – who had become Viscount Sidmouth – and Canning.

DISCIPLES CATCHING THE MANTLE, 1808

The general political confusion that followed Pitt's death lasted for a considerable time. This cartoon was drawn two years later, when no clear successor had emerged. Gillray repays the many commissions that he had received from Canning by making him the favourite; but Canning had to wait *nineteen years before becoming Prime Minister. The Opposition is condemned to outer darkness. The Biblical reference is to Elijah's mantle falling upon Elisha. In 1817, when the radical pamphleteer, Henry Hone, was tried for seditious blasphemy, he produced this print to show that the great Gillray had parodied the Scriptures in the interests of the Government of the day.*

THE LAST GRAND MINISTERIAL EXPEDITION, 1810

*I*n 1810 the Government, led by Spencer Perceval, was so worried about the prospect of political unrest that it took action in the Court to restrict the freedom of the press. The radical MP, Sir Francis Burdett, took up the cause of the press and was condemned by the House of Commons, which went so far as to commit him to custody. The Sergeant at Arms was prevented from doing so by the huge crowds that gathered around Burdett's house in Piccadilly. The following day, the Horse Guards were called out to arrest Burdett. The leader of this repressive expedition is seen to be Perceval, who wears the robes of the Chancellor of the Exchequer. The irony of this cartoon by Isaac Cruikshank is that the Government was being lambasted at that time for the miserable failure of the naval expedition to Walcheren in the Low Countries in the previous year. The only campaign that Perceval could win was to arrest an MP at his house in central London.

MR PERCEVAL ASSASSINATED IN THE LOBBY OF THE HOUSE OF COMMONS BY JOHN BELLINGHAM, 11 MAY 1812

*C*learly, the murder of a Prime Minister was too appalling to portray in caricature. This drawing is by Charles Williams, a prolific cartoonist who started very much in the tradition of Gillray, but whose later work diminished into realism.

THE PRIME CRUTCH – LORD LIVERPOOL

George Cruikshank, son of Isaac, made some woodcuts for the satirical magazines published by William Hunt, 1819–20. They are some of his best caricatures. Here he emphasizes the extraordinary walnut-shaped profile of one of Britain's least-known but longest-serving Prime Ministers.

'He knows not what it is to feel within
A comprehensive faculty, that grasps
Great purposes with ease, that turns
    and wheels,
Almost without an effort, plans too
    vast
For his conception, which he cannot
    move.'
William Cowper

THE ROYAL DOCKYARD, 1814

A detail from a cartoon by George Cruikshank. Lord Liverpool is one of a number of ministers playing with boats made from walnut shells. He is not in charge, but at least he has a tub of his own for his toys – an allusion, perhaps, to the great maritime bustling city from which his title was taken.

Liverpool was lucky that after 1820 cartoonists were less savage. George Cruikshank (1792–1878), who started to draw in 1810, was in the sharply acerbic tradition. But after 1820 his political sharpness softened and, preferring to draw social cartoons, he turned to book illustration, most notably for *Oliver Twist* (1837). There was no Gillray, Dent or Newton for the next seventy years and Prime Ministers were to get off pretty lightly.

A RADICAL REFORMER, 1819

In 1819 the economic crisis inflamed political unrest. In the cheap press there were calls for armed resistance to the Government; the Church and clergy were openly attacked; and the Radical Reformers demanded universal suffrage. In August the Manchester Yeomanry rode into a large meeting of 50,000 people at St Peter's Fields in Manchester, killing 11 and wounding 400 people – the Peterloo Massacre. Liverpool's Government reacted by introducing six Bills designed to repress public protest. In this cartoon by George Cruikshank, the Radical Reformers are seen to be introducing revolution, complete with the guillotine. Castlereagh flees before the monster and Liverpool falls across a bag full of gold coins.

A SCENE IN THE NEW FARCE OF THE LADY AND THE DEVIL, 1820

*T*he first crisis of the new reign was the reappearance of George IV's estranged wife, Caroline, who demanded to be crowned Queen. It dominated the political world. Some politicians, like Brougham, took up the side of the Queen; others, like Liverpool, that of the King. The scene describes the effect upon the King and the inner Cabinet of the news that Caroline had at last landed in England. The figure in the centre, with the walnut-shaped face, is Lord Liverpool.

This cartoon, probably by Isaac Cruikshank, uses the technique of deliberately lengthening the faces of all the participants, which became fashionable for a short time.

7 · Reform

April 1827: George Canning
August 1827: 1st Viscount Goderich (later 1st Earl of Ripon)
January 1828: 1st Duke of Wellington. *November 1830:* 2nd Earl Grey
May 1832: 1st Duke of Wellington. *May 1832:* 2nd Earl Grey
July 1834: Viscount Melbourne. *December 1834:* Sir Robert Peel
April 1835–September 1841: Viscount Melbourne

O N 18 February 1827, Lord Liverpool had a stroke. For some time it was not clear whether he would make a full recovery. Even when that possibility receded, it was exceedingly difficult to decide on a successor. In the end, six weeks after Liverpool's stroke, George IV chose Canning.

Canning brought style and vigour to a dull Government. He had linked himself to Pitt in the 1790s, but had always been looked upon as a bit of an outsider. He was the son of an actress and the Whig Earl Grey dismissed his pretensions by saying, 'The son of an actress is ipso facto disqualified from being Prime Minister.' Canning had been a writer, poet and journalist, but politics was his first love, and he was able to finance his career by marrying an heiress. He was a great Foreign Secretary, and in South America was regarded as a hero since he encouraged the break-up of the Spanish Empire. In this connection he coined the memorable words, 'I called the New World into existence to redress the balance of the Old.'

The cartoonists, having struggled with Liverpool's lack of a recognizable persona, relished the fact that a vivid character had become Prime Minister, particularly one who was about to split his party. Most were favourable to Canning and he is easily recognized, for he is almost completely bald. He was also in office for a very short time. Canning had supported Catholic emancipation and many Tories, including the Duke of Wellington and Lord Eldon, refused to serve under him. This was recorded in a memorable cartoon, *The Funeral of Tory-Principle.* However, after a mere 100 days Canning succumbed to a wasting form of lumbago and died at the age of 57. It says much for his character that he inspired Peel, Palmerston, Gladstone and the young Disraeli.

THE STRUGGLE, OR A LONG PULL, 1827

The divided nature of the Tory Party: Canning rows one way under the flag 'Catholic Supremacy'; Eldon, the Lord Chancellor, rows the other way under 'Protestant Ascendancy'. Eldon had been Lord Chancellor for many years and so enjoyed office that he only very reluctantly surrendered his Seals.

The cartoon is by Henry Heath, possibly a brother of William (see p. 82), a popular caricaturist and generally favourable to Canning.

George IV then chose Viscount Goderich, the Chancellor of the Exchequer, to whom Cobbett had given the ironical nickname 'Prosperity Robinson' after he had cut tax substantially. Goderich was a stop-gap who failed to reconcile the differing views in the Tory Party over Catholic emancipation. He resigned before Parliament met – the only Prime Minister to do this – and became known as 'The Duke of Fuss and Bustle'. When he was appointed by George IV, he broke down and wept; the King called him a 'blubbering fool'. Goderich also wept when some ministers declined to serve: during his final interview with the King, George IV lent him his handkerchief. He features in few cartoons and is the least recognized of all 19th-Century Prime Ministers.

The King then turned to Wellington, whom he summoned to Windsor early one morning. George IV was in bed wearing a turban nightcap and said bluntly, 'Arthur, the Cabinet is defunct.'

Opposite
THE FUNERAL OF TORY-PRINCIPLE, APRIL 1827

*T*he leading Tories refuse to serve under Canning after Liverpool's illness. They are led by Eldon, with a handkerchief to his eyes, followed by Wellington and Peel, Melville in a Scotch cap, and Goulburn squinting. They were attacked for deserting Canning. The press and the City supported the Prime Minister and Catholic emancipation.

The cartoon is by 'H.B.', the initials used by John Doyle. He produced a large number of lithographs depicting historical events from the 1820s to the 1840s. Maclean, the publisher, advertised them as 'Entirely free from whatever could offend the most scrupulous or worry the most susceptible'.

Doyle's figures are accurate portrayals rather than caricatures and his comment is generally good-humoured. This new softer approach was helped by his use of lithography, rather than etching, which tended to soften the edges.

THE GAME COCK AND THE DUNGHILLS, 1827

*G*eorge IV appointed Canning as Prime Minister and he is shown by Henry Heath as the cock of the walk. Brougham encouraged the King to appoint him in a letter: 'Sir, your Father broke the domination of the Whigs; I hope Y.M. will not endure that of the Tories.' 'No, I'll be damned if I do', replied the King. So he is very happy in the window. Some of the old Tory Ministers are leaving, led by Wellington, who says, 'D.I.O.' – 'Damme! I'm Off'. Canning had to appoint a few Tories who remained loyal to him and some Whigs.

THE NATIONAL POP-SHOP
IN THREADNEEDLE STREET,
1826

*I*n this cartoon there are four Prime
Ministers. Liverpool, still in office, is
at the bottom of the ladder; Canning,
then the Foreign Secretary, is at the
top; Peel, the Home Secretary, supports
the ladder from the right; and
Robinson, wearing his Chancellor's
robes, supports it from the left.
Robinson is making a very rare
appearance; later, he was to become
Prime Minister as Viscount Goderich.
His obscurity made him elusive.

The financial crisis that occasioned
this cartoon by Robert Cruikshank
was caused by a run on the banks.
Liverpool and Robinson refused to
issue Exchequer Bills to relieve
commercial distress. Instead, they
wanted the banks to lend money –
hence the pawn shop – to those in
trouble.

THE FIELD OF BATTERSEA, 1829

*L*ord Winchilsea, a rabid Protestant, had alleged in a letter to a newspaper that Wellington had always been a closet supporter of Catholic emancipation. The Duke asked for an apology, which was not given, and a duel was arranged in Battersea Fields for the early hours of 21 March 1829. The Duke, who was a notoriously bad shot, fired at Winchilsea's legs and missed; Winchilsea fired into the air. His seconds produced a statement that did not include the word 'apology', but Wellington insisted upon it. When it was agreed, he touched his hat and bade everybody, 'Good Morning'.

This cartoon was by Paul Pry, the pseudonym of William Heath. He was an ex-captain of the Dragoons who became a popular caricaturist and book illustrator.

The Ultra Tories were pleased that Wellington had become Prime Minister, but they were about to experience one of the great U-turns of British politics. In 1828, a by-election in Ireland was won by Daniel O'Connell, who was a Roman Catholic and thus debarred from sitting in the House of Comons. It was clear that in the future many more Catholic MPs would be returned for Irish seats and in effect their constituencies would be disenfranchised. Ireland would have become ungovernable. Wellington and Peel therefore decided that constitutional and civil strife could only be avoided if Catholics were allowed to sit in Parliament; accordingly, they introduced Catholic emancipation.

PORTRAIT OF A NOBLE DUKE, 1829

Wellington was not only the most popular and best-known soldier, he was also Commander-in-Chief – a post he wanted to keep after he had become Prime Minister. Some of his enemies thought that he favoured a sort of military rule, but his Cabinet, in his absence, decided that he had to resign his military office. All the accoutrements of warfare – cannon, drums, sabres, field tents, flags and sentry boxes – are used to emphasize his military past rather than his democratic future.

GUY FAWKES, OR THE ANNIVERSARY OF THE POPISH PLOT, 1830

Lord Winchilsea got his revenge on Wellington by leading the Ultra Tories to vote down his Government in the House of Lords. Here he leads the Guy Fawkes procession, with Wellington as the Guy. At that time, 5 November was celebrated with strong anti-Catholic processions in many towns. The artist is H.B. (John Doyle).

Many never forgave Wellington, and one peer, Lord Winchilsea, challenged him to a duel. Wellington was the last Prime Minister to endure such an ordeal.

The next great issue was the reform of Parliament. In 1830 George IV died and was succeeded by his brother, William IV. In those days a General Election had to be held on the death of the sovereign, and Wellington's majority was reduced. Wellington was strongly opposed to reform and declared that, 'beginning Reform is beginning Revolution'. In the King's Speech he dismissed any idea of reform. The Ultras in the House of Lords, still bitter over Catholic emancipation, then decided to

THE TWO MEN IN THE GIG, 1831

In the Autumn of 1830, machine-breaking and rick-burning spread over southern England; even houses and barns were burned. Economic despair was also inflamed by radical magazines which demanded Parliamentary reform. Judges imposed severe sentences and rioters were hanged. In this rare cartoon by William Heath, Wellington is depicted as the black skeleton driven by Death himself.

strike by voting him down on an issue unrelated either to reform or to Catholics. This naked act of revenge rebounded upon them, for Wellington was replaced by a Whig Government committed to parliamentary reform.

Wellington's premiership of nearly three years saw the last great flurry of scurrilous cartooning. He was a gift to the cartoonists – the hooked nose, the uniforms, the aloof disdain and the boot were all endlessly featured. He often laughed at the cartoons, saying to his old friend, 'There is nothing but calumny in the world, Mrs Arbuthnot, and I must make up my mind to be exposed to it.'

Earl Grey then became Prime Minister at the age of 66. He had sat in one or other of the Houses of Parliament for 43 years and yet had only held office for a year in the 'Broad-Bottomed Ministry'. Now he was to pass into history as 'Lord Grey of the Reform Bill'. He appointed as ministers only Whigs, most of whom were landed noblemen: it is ironic that this radical Cabinet owned more acres than any earlier Cabinet.

THE LAST DAY OR THE FALL OF THE CHARLEYS, 1829

*T*he one thing that everyone knows about Robert Peel is that he founded the Metropolitan Police Force and gave his name, 'Bobby', to the constables. In September the first thousand of Peel's new police constables started to patrol in London, which meant that the old nightwatchmen, who were rather friendly and popular figures, were redundant. Peel was not at all popular for introducing the reform, which was attacked for being militaristic, autocratic and inquisitorial.

THE SCHOOL OF REFORM, 1831

*T*his print appeared at the beginning of the long crisis of Reform. Grey is portrayed as a schoolmaster patiently trying to teach the reluctant and stupid Tories how to conjugate the word 'reform'. Wellington, with a dunce's cap, is in the corner saying, 'I can't reform.' Only Peel looks at Grey.

C.J. Grant's prints had strong radical sympathies. He produced many woodcuts for broadsheets and the popular press, which were the lower end of the market. His woodcuts are strong and bold, and they all attack the Establishment.

LITTLE JOHNNY ROUSE-HELL OR THE MINISTERS LAST SHIFT, 1831

*L*ord *John Russell was the prime mover in the House of Commons for the three Reform Bills. Here he is depicted as a dangerous betrayer of ancient liberties who is consigning into Hell the Magna Carta and the Bill of Rights. As reform in the country was widely popular, anti-reform cartoons were much less common than pro-reform ones.*

THE ROYAL MOPSTICK, 1831

*T*his woodcut, by the radical C.J. Grant, portrays King William IV as the empty doll through which Grey speaks. Grey is issuing the King's speech to the House of Lords to prorogue Parliament. The real power of the Prime Minister was* demonstrated later when Grey persuaded the King to use the royal prerogative, if it should prove necessary, to create enough peers to form a pro-reform majority in the Lords. The result was to consolidate the constitutional practice of the sovereign acting upon the advice of his leading minister.*

THE MINISTRY THAT WOULD NOT DO, 1832

*I*n May 1832 Grey resigned after he had asked the King to create peers to carry the Reform Bill through the House of Lords and the King had declined to do so. William IV turned to the Duke of Wellington, but it took only three days for Wellington to realize that he could not form a Government. This clever cartoon underlines the repressive measures that would have had to have been taken if the Government were to survive. It was also a witty reminder of Wellington's past.

The artist, Robert Seymour, succeeded William Heath as the leading caricaturist in The Looking Glass, *but he became popular for his comic drawings of the misfortunes of cockney sportsmen. He also drew some of the plates for* Pickwick Papers *but overwork led to breakdown and suicide in 1836.*

In March 1831 the young Lord John Russell, later to be a Prime Minister himself, introduced a Bill to abolish sixty rotten boroughs that were in the gift of patrons and to extend the franchise considerably. It secured a majority of one in the Commons, but when the Lords defeated it Grey called an election. This was the first 'modern' election, for the overriding issue was parliamentary reform. Grey won a large majority. The second Bill was also rejected by the House of Lords in October. There were public meetings of protest and riots, while a mob broke the windows of Apsley House, the London home of the Duke of Wellington.

When a third Bill was rejected by the Lords in May 1832, Grey asked the King to create fifty peers to swamp the anti-government majority. Appalled at this, William IV asked Wellington to form a Government, but the Duke could not put one together that would command the confidence of the House of Commons. Grey therefore resumed the premiership and William IV let it be known that he would create a sufficient number of peers if necessary. Wellington realized that the game was up and told his supporters to abstain. The Bill was passed in 1832.

Only one in eight adult males received the vote, but the resulting Act marked the end of the old order. Peel thought that it was the most important Act passed by Parliament for a hundred years. It set Britain down the road to universal suffrage. The first steps had been taken in the formation of the political parties that were to dominate the 19th and 20th Centuries. In the 1831 General Election the word 'Conservative' came into general use to describe the opponents of reform. The reformers have often been called Liberals, though the word was not generally used by contemporaries.

LORK, WHAT A LONG TAIL OUR CAT HAS GOT, 1831

On the whole, Grey is treated well at the hands of the cartoonists. But here William Heath could not resist a sly dig about his use of patronage. The tail of the cat lists all the jobs that were in his gift and that his relations had. His son, sons-in-law, brothers, brothers-in-law and umpteen cousins were all aboard the gravy train.

A CABINET COUNCIL, 1834

When Melbourne resigned, Peel was in Rome and so Wellington 'took over' the Government for ten days. He drove around each of the main departments dealing with their business. As soon as Peel returned, Wellington stood down. H.B. (John Doyle) is the cartoonist.

The cartoonists loved this constitutional crisis. Grey and Russell are usually depicted as the heroes, Wellington and the Tories as the diehards. There is much less caricature and venom than before: the figures are more like portraits. The leading cartoonist of the 1830s was John Doyle (1797–1868), who published a large number of cartoons under the initials H.B. He softened cartooning, a process that was to be continued by John Leech (1817–64) and Sir John Tenniel (1820–1914). Cartoons were no longer individual prints bought by the political elite; from then on they appeared in newspapers and satirical periodicals seen by millions. The editors did not want to offend the taste of their new readers and so the cartoons had to be acceptable in the Victorian family drawing-room. British cartoon art was about to enter a long period of respectable dullness.

One of the beneficiaries of this was Lord Melbourne, who became Prime Minister in 1834 after Grey's resignation. He was a handsome and worldly man, but his flirtations did not appear much in the cartoons. When he was cited in a divorce action, virtually no cartoonists referred to this incident.

Melbourne was splendidly idle. Disraeli described him as 'sauntering over the destinies of the Nation, and lounging among the glories of Empire'. His regular question when policy matters were put to him was, 'Why can't you leave it alone?', for he believed that 'all that Government has to do is to prevent and punish crime'. None of this natural indolence came through in the cartoons.

Melbourne soon ran into serious difficulties and after a few months resigned – to the relief of the King, who preferred the Tories. Wellington had no wish to be Prime Minister again and Peel was the obvious choice. He was on holiday in Rome and so Wellington had to stand in, holding

TWO TURTLE DOVES, 1835

TURTLE DOVES *in the* BIRD CAGE WALK,
or PURE INNOSENSE

*T*his is a rare cartoon – so rare that the British Museum does not have a copy – alluding to the alleged affair between Melbourne and Mrs Norton. Mrs Norton was the pretty, twenty-year-old wife of a Conservative MP. The Nortons lived in Storey's Gate and their garden backed onto Birdcage Walk, which was just a few minutes from the House of Lords. Melbourne and Mrs Norton exchanged intimate letters, which revealed that he had an abiding interest in flagellation. In spite of the fact that Melbourne gave Norton a Judgeship in the Metropolitan Police Courts, he sought divorce.

Norton, however, was unable to produce any evidence apart from some anodoyne letters. The young Charles Dickens reported the case for the Morning Chronicle *and used Norton's Counsel as the model for Sergeant Buzfuz who, in the famous trial of* Bardell v Pickwick, *also had little evidence. Norton lost; Melbourne always protested his innocence.*

THE FAERY QUEENE, 1838

*T*he Queen is mounted on Peel, who is led by Melbourne, while Russell waits in the background. H.B. (John Doyle) describes the extraordinary 'Bedchamber Crisis' of 1838. When Melbourne was defeated in the House of Lords over a colonial dispute, he resigned. Peel tried to form a Government, but he insisted that the Queen should dismiss certain Whig ladies from her Household. Victoria refused: Peel resigned; and Melbourne was recalled. This soured the Queen's relationship with Peel and she always looked upon him as a cold fish. Melbourne often appears in cartoons as a lamb, as that was his family name.

SUSANNAH AND THE ELDERS, 1837

William IV died in 1837 and was succeeded by his 18-year-old niece, Victoria. Melbourne gave her a great deal of valuable political and worldly advice. In her diary for Christmas Day 1839, she says that Melbourne 'was the one whom I look up to as a father'. This cartoon by H.B. (John Doyle) shows the young and innocent Queen flanked by Melbourne and Palmerston, both notorious lechers. On her left is the Foreign Secretary, Palmerston. Ironically, they were men of the world; both, as Prime Ministers, were cited in divorce actions.

all the Offices of State for about ten days. Peel called an election and issued his famous Tamworth Manifesto, the first time that a political programme had been put to the electorate, pledging his party to 'Conservative' reform. It was apparently successful, for the Conservatives won over a hundred seats; but they failed to secure an overall majority. Peel did not resign at once, but was driven out when he was defeated in the House of Commons six times in six weeks.

William IV had to recall Melbourne, who was therefore still Prime Minister when Victoria succeeded to the throne at the age of eighteen in 1837. He assumed the role of a favoured old uncle, riding beside her, giving advice and dining with her three or four times a week. She said, 'I look upon him as a father.' She repaid this kindness in the 1840s when Melbourne got into financial difficulties. He actually had to turn down the Garter because accepting it involved an outlay of £1,000. He told the Queen of his financial problems and she personally lent him sufficient to get him through.

8 · The Hungry Forties

PRIME MINISTERS

September 1841: Sir Robert Peel (2nd Ministry)

July 1846–February 1852: Lord John Russell (later Earl Russell)

THERE COULD be no greater contrast than between Melbourne, the 18th-Century Whig from the landed aristocracy, and Robert Peel, the son of a cotton-spinning industrialist from Lancashire. This very rich businessman bought his son a rotten borough in Ireland in 1809 and three years later Liverpool made the young Peel the Irish Secretary. In this position his strongly anti-Catholic views earned him the first of many nicknames, 'Orange Peel'.

He was an exceptionally able administrator, determined to get on with the good government of the country, whether by creating the Metropolitan Police as Home Secretary in the 1820s, or by balancing the nation's finances as Prime Minister. Not a great original thinker, Peel changed his views as the conditions of the moment required. Originally opposed to Catholic emancipation, he legislated to introduce it when he was convinced that civil order was threatened. He opposed parliamentary reform, but when the measure was carried, he accepted it and made no attempt at repeal. Walter Bagehot, the editor of the *Economist*, said of him: 'of all the great measures with which his name is associated he attained great eminence as an opponent before he attained even greater eminence as their advocate'.

Nowhere was this more true than in the repeal of the Corn Laws, which had greatly restricted the importation of foreign grain and had been introduced in 1815 to protect British farming. Bread was the staple diet and the principal item of expenditure for the working classes; high corn prices often meant starvation. From 1836 the campaign for the repeal of the Corn Laws was started and the Anti-Corn Law League was founded by Richard Cobden and John Bright in 1839. The parties were divided and some good harvests in the early 1840s pushed the question back a little.

But failure of the potato crop in Ireland and the bad harvest of 1845 persuaded Peel that the duties should go. His supporters claim that this commitment to Free Trade was the foundation of Victorian prosperity

A PLAUSIBLE PLEA, 1842

Peel took personal charge of the 1842 Budget, in which he restored Income Tax. Here he presents the Income Tax Bill to Palmerston, who was in opposition. In 1840, 'Pam', as Foreign Secretary, had played a major part in starting the Opium War against China. This continued across the change of Government and eventually led to a treaty in 1842 under which Hong Kong was ceded to Britain. A large sum of money was also paid by China. In this cartoon Peel is told not to present his Bill for Income Tax to the British people, but to get the money from the spoils of the China War.

THE QUEEN'S 'SEVENPENCE', 1842

*P*eel inherited a Budget deficit from Melbourne. Four-fifths of the Government's revenue came from Customs and Excise duties on a wide range of goods. Peel decided to reduce these, while introducing Income Tax at seven pence in the pound on all incomes over £150 a year. Pitt had levied Income Tax to pay for the French Wars, but it had been repealed in 1816. Here Peel is shown collecting from the Queen, though Albert does not look too happy. Income Tax soon became as unpopular as the old Customs duties and it had to be renewed every three years. By the time Peel left office, he had created a surplus and repaid some of the national debt.

A HIGHLAND REEL, 1842

*I*n 1842, Queen Victoria visited Scotland for the first time with Prince Albert. Peel was in attendance and clearly did not like it at all. He was always a little uneasy with the Queen. The artist is H.B. (John Doyle).

94 *The Hungry Forties*

THE POLITICAL PECKSNIFF, 1843

The readers of Punch *were the literate middle classes and they would have appreciated the literary allusion in this cartoon. In 1843–44, Charles Dickens published his novel* Martin Chuzzlewit *with his famous portrayal of the hypocritical architect, Pecksniff, who was 'like a signpost, always pointing the way but never going'. Halbot K. Browne's drawing of Pecksniff was an inspired comic illustration and is copied here with Peel's face. Dickens had been a parliamentary reporter and must have heard Peel speak in the House of Commons in the early 1830s. He could well have based his famous creation upon him.*

and prevented revolution. In his own words it was, 'the best measure to avert a great calamity'.

Nevertheless, it had devastating political consequences, for it split the Conservative Party - 231 Tory MPs voted against repeal. It kept them from office for over twenty years. Disraeli was vicious about Peel's lack of principle, which 'established political infidelity throughout the land'.

There was a cool reserve about Peel. Victoria confided to her diary in 1839 that he was 'such a cold, odd man'; Daniel O'Connell more piquantly said that, 'his smile was like the plate on a coffin'. But he was much more savaged by the orators in the House of Commons than by the cartoonists. *Punch* started in 1841 and Leech, its main political cartoonist, drew him as a distinguished figure. But before the days of photography, few people would have recognized him. That fact saved his life, for his secretary was killed by someone who mistook him for Peel.

Gladstone considered that Peel was the greatest Prime Minister of the 19th Century. The poor of the industrial cities had a champion; at his death from a riding accident on Constitution Hill, *Punch* carried a cartoon of a monumental pyramid of loaves. In 1846 the Repeal of the Corn Laws was carried by the 'Peelite' Conservatives with the support of the Whig Opposition. On the same night, Peel was defeated on a separate issue and resigned. The reality was that he could no longer hold the Conservative Party together. Lord John Russell, famous for his campaign on the Reform Act of 1832, took over.

Lord Russell was the last Prime Minister who can undoubtedly be called a Whig. He came from one of the great aristocratic families who had supported the Revolution of 1688 and this inspired him more than anything else. He was a passionate lover of civil liberty and believed that once reform had been passed the newly enfranchised middle classes would still give pride of place to noble families such as his own. He had little interest in schemes for social improvement, but had blind faith that by continuing parliamentary reform things would get better. Russell was

YOUNG GULLIVER AND THE BROBDIGNAG MINISTER, 1845

*D*israeli *had asked for office under Peel, but had been offered nothing. He became Peel's most vicious critic, uttering the most devastating attacks in the House of Commons with a sarcastic drawl and an impassive* countenance. *In 1845, he ended one speech:*

> '*Dissolve if you please the Parliament you have betrayed, and appeal to the people who, I believe, mistrust you. For me there remains this at least the opportunity of expressing thus publicly my belief that a Conservative Government is an Organised Hypocrisy.*'

STAG AT BAY, 1846

Here, H.B. (John Doyle) uses Landseer's famous painting of the Stag at Bay to describe Peel's savaging by Bentinck and Disraeli, who were leading members of his own Party. Bentinck had been an MP for 18 years and had been offered a place by Peel in 1841, but he could not spare time from his passion for racing. However, he gave that up to fight Peel. He helped Disraeli, who had little spare money, to buy a country estate, Hughenden, in Buckinghamshire, making him a country gentleman. Two years later he died suddenly, leaving the leadership in the Commons to Disraeli. Wellington called the alliance against Peel 'a blackguard combination', but it succeeded – the stag was brought down and the Tories faced two decades in the wilderness.*

very short and the cartoonists as early as 1831 enjoyed commenting on this. Sidney Smith, the great Whig and wit, wrote in a letter, 'I met John Russell at Exeter. The people all along the road were very much disappointed at this smallness. I told them he was much larger before the Bill was thrown out but was reduced by excessive anxiety about the people. This brought tears to their eyes.'

Russell also looked like a little terrier, a Jack Russell, and that is how the cartoonists sometimes depicted him. The period from 1846 to 1868 was the heyday of the House of Commons. Parliamentary votes, in the absence of a properly organized party whipping system, meant that support for each measure had to be awkwardly engineered. Disraeli was dismissive of this system and said that each Bill was 'altered, remoulded, re-modelled, patched, cobbled, painted, veneered, and varnished'.

PUNCH'S MONUMENT TO PEEL, 1850

In 1850, Peel was thrown by his horse while riding on Constitution Hill; his lung was crushed. He lingered on in considerable pain for three days. Following his death, money was collected around the country to erect monuments to him and Punch *published this monument of 'Loaves to the Poor'. In the debate in 1846, Peel had defended his famous U-turn when he abandoned protection by repealing the Corn Laws: 'I shall leave a name execrated by every monopolist who clamours for protection . . . but it may be that I shall leave a name, sometimes remembered with expressions of goodwill in the abodes of those whose lot it is to labour and to earn their daily bread by the sweat of their brow, when they shall recruit their exhausted strength with abundant and untaxed food.'*

Russell was kept in office by the mutual hatred of the two wings of the Conservative Party – the Peelites, who supported Free Trade, ranged against the Protectionists, who represented the country and landed interests. In the late 1840s, Benjamin Disraeli became leader of the Conservatives in the House of Commons. He set about using his novels and his theatrical oratory to give new heart to a demoralized and defeated party.

The strongest character in Russell's government was Viscount Palmerston, the Foreign Secretary. He conducted British foreign policy largely on his own. In 1851 he supported the *coup d'état* by Louis Napoleon, who was later to become Napoleon III. Russell could not stomach that, and dismissed him. Two months later, Palmerston got his revenge by supporting an Opposition motion vote that put Russell out of office.

POLITICAL ECONOMY; OR, LORD JOHN IN PEEL'S CLOTHES, 1846

*L*ord John Russell's shortness was a gift for the cartoonists. He did not have Peel's political stature either. A piece of doggerel summed up his distant coolness:

'Like or dislike, he does not give a jot:
He wants your votes, but your
    affections not,
Yet human hearts need sun as well as
    oats
So cold a climate plays the deuce with
    votes.'

THE CHARTER, 1848

*T*he working-class movement to obtain six reforms through a Charter – universal male suffrage, annual Parliaments, the payment of MPs, secret ballots, equal electoral districts and the removal of property qualifications for MPs – had been in existence for twelve years. It reached its peak in 1848, the famous year of revolutions in Europe. Russell resisted this pressure. He banned a great rally in London and brought in troops to stand by. The Chartist movement fizzled out and reform came in a piecemeal way. Wellington was, after all, probably right when he said that the people of England were 'very quiet'. At that time, Punch had not shaken off its radical leanings and favoured the Chartists.

9 · Partyless Government

RUSSELL was followed by a Conservative, the Earl of Derby. His father had bought him the rotten borough of Stockbridge for his 21st birthday and he had begun his career as a Whig serving in Grey's Government. He moved over to the Tories and was a strong opponent of Free Trade. But he also spent much of his time at his great country house, Knowsley in Lancashire, shooting, racing and writing a rather good translation of *The Iliad*. Derby was not the only serious student of Homer among Prime Ministers: Chatham died in the arms of the Younger Pitt, who had been reading him *The Iliad*. Gladstone was always dipping into Homer and wrote books about him. Derby's friend, Bulwer Lytton coined the description that has stuck:

> *The brilliant chief, irregularly great*
> *Frank, haughty, rash, the Rupert of Debate.*

In 1852 Disraeli was surprised to be offered the Chancellorship of the Exchequer. He protested that he did not know anything about finance, to which Derby replied, 'You know as much as Mr Canning did, they give you the figures.' This short administration was known as the 'Who Who Government' since the Duke of Wellington, who was very deaf, asked after each name mentioned in the Cabinet – and it included some very obscure people – 'Who? Who?'

100

THE PROTECTION GIANT, 1852

*F*ollowing Russell's defeat, Derby and Disraeli tried to form a Government, but it only lasted until December. This cartoon shows the Derby Government was two-headed – Disraeli, who was about to abandon his objection to Free Trade, and Derby, who did not really understand economics and was ambivalent. It was said that the Tories were 'Protectionists in the counties, fence-sitters in small towns, and Free Traders in the cities'. As a result, the two-headed giant did not attack the citadel of Free Trade, whose defender is not a leader of the former Government, but Richard Cobden, who never held ministerial office.

HIT HIM AGAIN! HE HAS NO FRIENDS!, 1852

*I*n his Budget, Disraeli proposed to increase the House Tax and to leave Income Tax alone. Punch, *still a fairly radical magazine, opposed the increase, which fell particularly heavily upon relatively poor people. In this cartoon, the Prime Minister, Derby, encourages his Chancellor, Disraeli, to hit a poor clerical worker, who in those days would probably not have had a vote.*

Disraeli presented his Budget with a five-hour speech that ended at one o'clock in the morning. Although Disraeli sat down to loud cheers,

Gladstone – the greatest Chancellor of the Exchequer in the 19th Century – rose and demolished it in a brilliant speech. The vote was taken at four o'clock and the Government was defeated. In the new administration, Gladstone became Chancellor and immediately he and Disraeli fell out. It was customary for the incoming Chancellor to buy the furniture at No. 11 Downing Street from his predecessor, but Gladstone declined, arguing that the State should provide the furniture and buy it from Disraeli. Disraeli also refused to hand over the Chancellor's robes; they had belonged to Pitt and he could not bear to see them worn by Gladstone.

"If he wags his tail it's all over with me."

THE BRITISH LION.

PUBLIC OPINION

DONE BY A SAXON 1854

ABERDEEN – PREMIER LION TAMER TO HRH PRINCE AL....T, 1854

*A*berdeen was attacked by Disraeli *in* The Press, '*His manner, arrogant and yet timid – his words insolent and yet obscure – offend even his political supporters.*' *At the bottom of society, one of the broadsheets sold in the streets spoke for the people:*

'*Yes our brave are dying,*
Coop'd up in heated camps
Before they well can strike a blow
At Russia's rugged scamps:
And as with furrowed brows they ask
"*What do our generals mean?*"
They curse, within their heart of hearts
"*That coward, ABERDEEN!*"'

In this cartoon by A. Saxon (presumably a pseudonym), Aberdeen has his head in the mouth of the British Lion, whose tail is labelled, 'Public Opinion'. The Prime Minister is saying, 'If he wags his tail, it's all over with me.'

Derby's Government was defeated over Disraeli's Budget, which increased Income Tax, and was savagely attacked by Gladstone – the first major clash of the Titans. Cartoonists often depicted Derby wearing a coronet and glasses; they had great fun contrasting the two leading Tories, who were known as 'The Jockey and the Jew'.

In 1852 Derby was succeeded by the 68-year-old Earl of Aberdeen, who presided over a coalition of Liberals and Peelites. He was a melancholy figure who always wore black clothes. He had had a tragically unhappy life, for his first wife had died young of a tubercular condition and their three daughters also died of the same disease – one of them in his own arms. He had met both Pitt and Napoleon, and through witnessing the battles that led up to Waterloo he became vehemently opposed to war. It was his misfortune, however, to be at No. 10 as Britain drifted into the Crimean War. Russia was interested in acquiring parts of the vast and sprawling Ottoman Empire as it started to break up. Many people in Britain came to see Russia as their country's most formidable rival and the Russian Bear was thought also to have designs upon India.

When William Russell's reports from the Crimea were published by *The Times*, they revealed massive incompetence and had a devastating effect. This is the only occasion in the history of the Premiership when a Prime Minister is forced to resign by a journalist. Aberdeen, who was called 'an antiquated imbecility', became very unpopular through his reluctance to pursue the war vigorously. In 1855, the House of Commons voted to set up an inquiry into the conduct of the war. Aberdeen had to resign and make way for Palmerston, another aged figure in his seventieth year. Bright commented that 50,000 Englishmen had died to make Palmerston Prime Minister.

There were by now regular, weekly political cartoons in *Punch*, which generally portrayed the main politicians as statesmen. Palmerston was usually drawn as a rather spunky character, riding horses over fences, while Aberdeen was portrayed as an old woman who did not know what to do.

Palmerston became Prime Minister after forty years experience in office. He had had a remarkable political career, for there were only two long Governments between 1807 and 1852 in which he took no part. Yet Disraeli described him as 'an imposter, utterly exhausted, at the best only ginger beer and not champagne, now an old painted pantaloon, very deaf, very blind and with false teeth that would fall out of his mouth when speaking, if he did not halt or hesitate in his talk.'

Palmerston's foreign policy was brutally simple. In 1848, he told the House of Commons, 'The furtherance of British interest should be the only object of a British Foreign Secretary.' For him, it was always Britain first; if necessary, he would dispatch a gunboat to protect the Imperial interest. He had no fixed party affiliation and earned himself a number of nicknames, such as 'Lord Cupid' and 'Lord Pumice-stone'. Towards the end of his life he was widely seen as the personification of England, and was endearingly known as 'Old Pam'. Gladstone later told a story about a meeting between Palmerston and a Frenchman who wanted to flatter him. The Frenchman said, 'If I was not a Frenchman, I would like

YOU ARE REQUESTED NOT TO SPEAK TO THE MAN AT THE WHEEL, 1855

*A*berdeen had a tough time at the hands of the cartoonists, who lambasted his relaxed and uncommitted handling of the Crimean War. Like Anthony Eden, he had been a famous Foreign Secretary under a strong Prime Minister – in his case, Peel and in Eden's case, Churchill – but both failed to live up to the demanding requirements of leading the nation themselves.

This cartoon was drawn by John Leech, who did over 300 political cartoons for Punch, *though he was much more renowned for his social and sporting drawings – on which he much preferred to work. Every week there was a meeting around the* Punch *table at which the line for the political cartoon was agreed; then Leech went away to draw it. He only used his own ideas on about ten occasions.*

CUPID, 1838

*T*his drawing of Palmerston as Cupid appeared in the satirical magazine, Figaro in London, *which circulated in the 1830s, and was a rare cartoon comment upon Palmerston's persistent philandering. In 1839, at the age of 55 and just about to get married, he took a fancy to Mrs Brand, one of the Queen's ladies-in-waiting at Windsor, and entered her bedroom. She resisted and told the Queen. Melbourne, Palmerston's brother-in-law, had to sweep the scandal under the carpet. Pam's luck had held again.*

THE STATE BUTLER GETS UP ANOTHER BOTTLE OF FINE OLD SMOKE, 1857

Palmerston had just produced a dull Queen's Speech because he was more interested in foreign affairs and deeply suspicious of undertaking any measures of reform. He managed to get away with this for over ten years.

WEIGHING FOR 'THE FAVOURITE', 1855

In the 1850s, Palmerston was on bad terms with Victoria and Albert. For a short time he was Home Secretary in Aberdeen's Government. Albert advised the Prime Minister to get rid of him and also to spread malicious reports about him. When Aberdeen resigned in 1855, the Queen asked four other ministers to form a Government. They could not; so, reluctantly, she sent for Palmerston. Not even Prince Albert could stop this and Palmerston wrote to his brother, 'I am, for the moment, l'inevitable.'

Although Palmerton was 70 in 1855, he was remarkably fit. His interests were politics, women and horses and this cartoon alludes to his sporting interests. In 1860 he had a runner in the Derby, which was third in the betting, and Pam himself rode down from Piccadilly to Epsom to watch the race. He didn't win. His trainer, Day, visited him in the House of Commons and Palmerston left a debate on Ireland to see him in the Lobby. When Day congratulated him on becoming Prime Minister again, Pam replied, 'Oh thanks John, I have won my Derby.'

At the age of 78, he bought a new pink hunting jacket and later celebrated his 80th birthday with a long ride over the Portsdown Hills in Dorset.

A LESSON IN DIP-LOMACY, 1865

This is one of the last cartoons of Palmerston, probably the first occasion on which a Prime Minister is shown wearing swimming trunks. It shows Palmerston as a vigorous 80-year-old who has just won an election and is ready to take a dip in the sea. Lord John Russell, who had then become Earl Russell and the Foreign Secretary, did not have Pam's grasp or panache and is floundering out of his depth. Readers would have remembered that 13 years earlier Russell had sacked Palmerston as Foreign Secretary, but within months Palmerston had engineered Russell's defeat in the House of Commons – the famous 'tit for tat' (see p. 98).

to be an Englishman', to which Palmerston replied, 'How strange. If I were not an Englishman, I would like to be an Englishman.'

Palmerston's period at No. 10 was disrupted for a year in 1858–59 when Derby became Prime Minister. Derby was turned out over the issue of parliamentary reform – a subject in which Palmerston had little interest. Palmerston believed that the British constitution was the best in the world, based on a Monarch, one House which contained the greatest landlords in the country, and a second House elected by 5 per cent of the male population. His last Government was dominated by his Chancellor of the Exchequer, William Gladstone, who was soon to become the leading figure of the Liberal Party. But Palmerston feared Gladstone's destructive force and said that later there would be trouble: 'he is a dangerous man and will run wild.'

Palmerston was one of the most colourful of Victoria's Prime Ministers. In the first twenty years of the 19th Century, the most famous club in London was Almack's, whose members had to be nominated by the opposite sex. 'Old Pam' was at home there, for three of the seven patronesses were reputed to be his mistresses. They included the young and beautiful Lady Jersey; the Countess of Lieven, who had been Metternich's mistress; and Lady Cowper, Melbourne's sister, whom

POLITICAL KIDNAPPING, 1867

*D*erby seizes the infant 'Reform' from Russell. Eight months after Derby formed his third administration, the Queen's speech in February 1867 indicated that there would be measures which 'without unduly disturbing the balance of political power, shall freely extend the electoral franchise'.

Palmerston later married when they were both in their fifties. Harriet Wilson, one of the high-class harlots of the day, recorded that Palmerston gave her money though did not say for what. He really did earn the sobriquet 'Lord Cupid'.

In 1863, in his 80th year, Palmerston was cited in a divorce action brought by a certain Timothy O'Kane, who claimed £20,000 damages. It was a complete try-on and although Gladstone was very distressed about the affair, Disraeli thought it would only do 'Old Pam' good. When the action was dismissed, cheering broke out in the Court and a few months later Palmerston increased his majority at the General Election. The wits at the time said, 'We all know about Kane but was Palmerston able?'

When Palmerston died in 1865, just after winning an election, Victoria asked Russell to form a Government – his third. It lasted a year and was brought down over reform. Russell had proposed to increase the electorate by 400,000, which was far too radical for the Conservatives who voted against it.

Derby then formed his third administration. It also addressed the reform issue, which by then had become the major political question, with vast public meetings being held across the country. The upshot was the Second Reform Act, which Disraeli steered through the Commons. Ironically, it was more radical than any of the earlier proposals that had been rejected. It greatly increased the electorate and made working men the overwhelming majority of voters in many constituencies. Derby called it 'A Leap in the Dark'.

A LEAP IN THE DARK, 1867

*I*n Derby's last Government, Disraeli
introduced 'Household Suffrage' as
the main proposal in his Reform Bill.
He had never been much interested in
reform and he proposed many
exclusions from that principle. In May,
the Marquess of Salisbury, a leading
member of the Government, and three
other Tories resigned. It was clear that
either the Government or the Bill
would have to go. Disraeli responded
by reducing the number of exclusions,
the effect of which was to increase the
electorate by more than one million
votes. This was twice as much as

Gladstone had proposed a year earlier
– at which time Disraeli had voted
against it.

Derby dubbed this, 'A Leap in the
Dark'. Disraeli may have had some
misty vision that these new voters were
going to be Conservative, for he had
long had a romantic view of the
working classes; but he never denied
the view of a leading Liberal that he
did it 'to dish the Whigs'. It is one of
the ironies of history that although
Gladstone was converted to universal
suffrage in the early 1860s, it was his
great rival, Disraeli, who took this
important step in that direction.

10 · Disraeli and Gladstone

PRIME MINISTERS
February 1868: Benjamin Disraeli (1st Ministry)
December 1868: William Ewart Gladstone (1st Ministry)
February 1874–April 1880: Benjamin Disraeli (Earl of Beaconsfield, 1876) (2nd Ministry)

DERBY RETIRED in 1868, crippled by gout. For a few months only Disraeli was the Prime Minister. The electorate had been expanded considerably after the Reform Act of the previous year; in the General Election that followed, the Liberals, who were then led by Gladstone, won a majority of over 100.

Gladstone was a brilliant scholar, deeply read in classics and theology. On Judgment Day, he believed, he would have to defend all his thoughts and actions before God, so he must act accordingly. He was to be in public life for 61 years, holding the office of Chancellor of the Exchequer for twelve of them and the premiership for fourteen.

Gladstone's first Government, from 1868 to 1874, was one of the great reforming administrations of the 19th Century. Forster's Education Act laid the foundations for universal elementary education; Cardwell's army reforms abolished the purchase of commissions. The Government also introduced secret ballots; strengthened the legal basis of trade unions; disestablished the Irish Church; and fused the administration of Common Law and Equity.

But Gladstone was a poor manager of the House of Commons and by 1874 his government had annoyed many groups and interests by its incessant legislation. The Government was tired. Two years earlier, in 1872, Disraeli had castigated it with this scathing and memorable description:

The Ministers remind me of one of those marine landscapes not very uncommon on the coasts of South America. You behold a range of exhausted volcanoes. Not a flame flickers on a pallid crest. But the situation is still dangerous. There are occasional earthquakes, and ever and anon the dark rumblings of the sea.

AT LAST!, 1868

In February 1868 Derby resigned and recommended that the Queen should invite Disraeli to be Prime Minister.

Disraeli was delighted and said to those who congratulated him, 'Yes, I have climbed to the top of the greasy pole.'

*B*oth Disraeli and Gladstone were prolific writers. In 1869–70 Gladstone published Juventus Mundi – The Gods and Men of the Heroic Age and Disraeli, his novel, Lothair. Gladstone wrote 20 books – 7 on theology, 5 on politics, 4 on Homer. Disraeli wrote 13 novels and 4 historical works.

Tenniel replaced Leech as the main political cartoonist of Punch in 1864 and held that position for the following 36 years. It was he above all who created the significant weekly political cartoon. It became an institution. People turned to it because it was meant to sum up the national mood. Tenniel's style was rather stiff and formal, but it was much imitated by his contemporaries and many of his successors. He was famous, of course, for the drawings in Alice in Wonderland, a fruitful area of imitation to many other cartoonists.

The nature of politics had changed. There were by then two distinct parties – Conservative and Liberal. Each was organized professionally; each had its own distinctive policies and appealed to a mass electorate. Disraeli had appointed the first Conservative National Agent, who set up Central Office. A comparable organization also existed in the Liberal Party. The shape of 20th-Century politics was established.

Both Gladstone and Disraeli used the railways to campaign, holding mass rallies across the country in great cities such as Manchester, Birmingham, Newcastle and Edinburgh. Unlike most of their predecessors, they became nationally recognized figures. They were not just known from *Punch* and other journals, but also from their photographs.

In the election of 1874 Disraeli, in his 70th year, became Prime Minister for the second time. There was further reform of the law and of the trade unions. The Artisans Dwellings Act, the Sale of Food and Drugs Act, and the Public Health Act were all major measures, which helped to transform Victorian England into a more modern state. The effect of a Liberal Government under Gladstone and a Conservative Government under Disraeli was to continue the process of change.

THE BELLE OF THE SEASON, 1874

*A*nti-Semitism was never far from the surface in Victorian England. Disraeli was frequently depicted as Shylock, cringing in a dirty old gaberdine. In this cartoon, which appeared when he became Prime Minister in 1874, his Jewish looks and long nose are exaggerated. The more sophisticated commentators called him and his policies 'oriental'. Nevertheless, he had overcome the enormous disadvantage of belonging to an ethnic minority to reach the twin positions of Leader of the Conservative Party and Prime Minister.

MOSÉ IN EGITTO!!!, 1875

*T*he Suez Canal was opened in 1869. It cut the journey from Britain to India by several weeks; by 1875 four-fifths of its traffic was British. Most of the shares were held by French interests or by the French engineer, Ferdinand de Lesseps. The Khedive of Egypt held the rest, but was faced with bankruptcy and had to sell them. Disraeli was determined that they should not be bought by the French and he agreed to purchase them. As Parliament was not sitting, the money could not be found in the ordinary way, and so Disràeli asked Baron Rothschild to lend them the amount of £4 million. 'When do you want it?', asked the Baron. 'Tomorrow.' 'What is your security?' 'The British Government.' 'You shall have it.' This was a diplomatic coup – and a fine investment.

Disraeli and Gladstone 113

NEW CROWNS FOR OLD ONES, 1876

*D*israeli's special relationship with the Queen started in his first short premiership in 1868. Victoria wrote in her diary, 'He is full of poetry, romance, and chivalry. When he knelt down to kiss my hand, which he took in both his hands, he said, "In loving loyalty and faith".' Disraeli was following his own dictum – when it comes to royalty, lay it on with a trowel. He called her the Faery after Spenser's Faery Queen and Victoria allowed him to write to her in the first person. Making the Queen the Empress of a vast continent East of Suez was a tribute to Dizzy's romantic and oriental emotions. The Queen liked it, too. Later in the same year, Disraeli was created the Earl of Beaconsfield – one good turn deserved another.

Where they differed was in international affairs, for Disraeli decided to play a starring role on the European and Imperial stages. In 1876, Disraeli made Victoria Empress of India, which was not just a grand and empty title but a clear signal to Russia that Britain would defend its interests in India against any threats. The 'Eastern Question' came to dominate politics. Essentially, the 'Eastern Question', like the Crimean War, was concerned with what should happen to the Ottoman Empire, which was continuing to disintegrate. Disraeli was determined to stop Russia grabbing strategic parts of it and his policy was to bolster up Turkey.

Gladstone had resigned the leadership of the Liberals in 1875, but the atrocities inflicted by the Turks upon the Christian communities in the Balkans, particularly in Bulgaria, which were still part of the Ottoman Empire, brought him back into the centre of politics. He wanted separate Christian states in the Balkans: the 'People's William' took the case to the people. At the Congress of Berlin in 1878, the Great Powers agreed to the orderly break up of part of the Turkish Empire, but sought to stabilize the remainder. War with Russia was avoided. Disraeli called this 'Peace with Honour' and it was the high point of his premiership. In 1879, Gladstone

WOODMAN, SPARE THAT TREE!, 1877

*G*ladstone was so appalled by the atrocities of the Turks against Christians in Bulgaria that he returned to national politics with his pamphlet, The Bulgarian Horrors and the Question of the East. *This included the famous passage in which he urged that the Turks be driven out of their possessions 'bag and baggage'. He said to a friend, 'Good ends are rarely obtained in politics without passion.'*

This cartoon by Tenniel celebrates Gladstone's two-and-a-half hour speech in the House of Commons. At first the House was empty, but then it filled to listen to his passionate tirade. The young Arthur Balfour, who was

later to be a Prime Minister, said that Gladstone's oratory that night had never been equalled.

Gladstone courted unpopularity over his campaign, since the prevailing mood in the country was anti-Russia and pro-Turkey. The word 'Jingo' was added to the English language through the popular music-hall song:

'We don't want to fight, but by Jingo if we do,
We've got the men, we've got the ships, we've got the money too –
We've fought the Bear before, and while we're Britons true,
The Russians shall not have Constantinople!'

As time went on, many people came round to Gladstone's point of view.

LE CONGRÈS, 1878

*T*his French cartoon reflects the
major role played by Beaconsfield
at the Congress of Berlin, from which
he returned with 'Peace with Honour'.
Beaconsfield and Tsar Alexander III
are the principal players; each has a
pistol by his hand. The third player is
Francis Joseph of Austria-Hungary. In
the background stands W.H.
Waddington, the French representative,
clutching the infant Third Republic,
while Bismarck of Germany watches
the game impassively. He said of
Disraeli, 'That old Jew, that is the
man.' Turkey is the child whose views
are unimportant, but whose empire
provides the prizes for the players.

started the first modern political campaign in Midlothian by holding mass meetings every day for a fortnight, in which he attacked everything that Disraeli had done. His campaign, assisted by an agricultural recession, led to a sweeping Liberal victory in 1880.

Gladstone and Disraeli were appealing for the first time to something that was looking like a modern electorate. After 1867 there were many constituencies in which men in humble circumstances formed the majority of the electorate and from 1872 they could vote as they chose by secret ballot without fear of retribution from landlords, employers or customers.

During the period of the great Gladstone/Disraeli duel, most people who were interested in politics either thought Gladstone a hero and Disraeli a villain, or vice versa. Voters of all social classes began to range themselves behind those towering leaders and to identify themselves with the Parties which they were shaping.

The Conservative and Liberal Parties of today still cherish the traditions and principles that Disraeli and Gladstone established. For the first time since Pitt and Fox, Britain experienced a conflict between two people of extraordinary ability at the very centre of politics. It was around those two men that the modern pattern of government of one party and opposition of another party, eager to assume to office at a moment's notice, took shape.

116 *Disraeli and Gladstone*

A BAD EXAMPLE, 1878

*D*israeli and Gladstone looked upon
each other as frauds. Disraeli said
of Gladstone, 'A ceaseless Tartuffe
from the beginning'. Gladstone replied,
'Even in these sacred walls he could
not forget to play the hypocrite.'
Gladstone's campaign against Turkey
following the Bulgarian atrocities
produced a torrent of oratorical abuse
from both. Disraeli: 'A sophisticated
rhetorician, inebriated by the
exuberance of his own verbosity.'
Again, 'Posterity will do justice to that
unprincipled maniac Gladstone – an
extraordinary mixture of envy,
vindictiveness, hypocrisy, and
superstition'; and 'With one
commanding characteristic whether
preaching, praying, speechifying, or
scribbling – never a gentleman.'
Gladstone responded, 'The man more
false than his doctrine . . . he
demoralised public opinion, bargained
with diseased appetites, stimulated
passions, prejudices and selfish desires
that they might maintain his influence.'
Mr Punch was not amused with the
mud-slinging; but the division between
party loyalties at all levels was very
sharp indeed.

THE MIDLOTHIAN
CAMPAIGN, 1879–80

Gladstone decided to give up his seat at Greenwich and fight a by-election in the Conservative seat of Midlothian. Supported and financed by Lord Rosebery, he held huge meetings in Edinburgh in November 1879. The Scots, many of whom had never seen the Grand Old Man, flocked in thousands to hear the denunciations of Disraeli's expansionist grab for Empire – 'pestilent . . . disloyal . . . thoroughly subversive . . . false phantoms of glory.' He injected into everything his great moral fervour, the very thing which Disraeli kept out of politics. It was the first modern election campaign. It grabbed the attention of the country and he won the by-election. This contemporary pamphlet, printed for the Tories, got it wrong, for Gladstone was also victorious at the ensuing General Election.

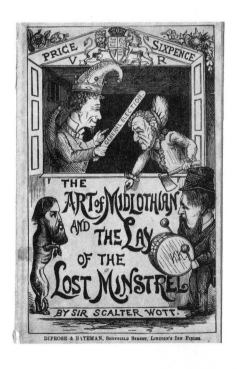

HIS LAST DECORATION, 1880

Disraeli's defeat was celebrated by J. Gordon Thomson in the satirical magazine, Fun, *which supported the Liberals. The Conservative magazine was* Judy, *but there were several others, including* Tomahawk, Funny Folk *and* Will o'the Wisp, *all of which carried political cartoons catering for the more literate middle-class electorate.*

Thomson was a civil servant when he started to draw for Punch *in the 1860s. He left the civil service in 1870 to become the political cartoonist for the Liberal* Fun. *His drawings are vigorous and imaginative.*

Disraeli and Gladstone 119

11 · 'Politics is Ireland'

PRIME MINISTERS

April 1880: W.E. Gladstone (2nd Ministry)
June 1885: 3rd Marquess of Salisbury (1st Ministry)
February 1886: W.E. Gladstone (3rd Ministry)
August 1886: 3rd Marquess of Salisbury (2nd Ministry)
August 1892: W.E. Gladstone (4th Ministry)
March 1894–June 1895: 5th Earl of Rosebery

GLADSTONE, at the age of 70, dominated the General Election of 1880 with his barnstorming Midlothian Campaign. The Liberals routed the Tories, but Gladstone was not the leader of his Party. The Queen abominated him, saying to her private secretary that she 'would sooner abdicate than send for or have anything to do with that half mad firebrand'. Disraeli advised Victoria to overlook his old arch-rival and send for Lord Hartington, a mild Whig. Within days it was clear that it had to be Gladstone. Not even Queen Victoria could set aside the people's choice.

Like most administrations of the late 19th Century, Gladstone's government had no clear programme and it was soon overwhelmed by events. Gladstone had launched his fiery oratory against Imperial expansion and Jingoism, but he was forced to bombard Alexandria. This led to Egypt being bought under British influence from 1882. It was to be Gladstone's undoing.

CABINET PICTURES, 1880

This was a nice comment by J. Gordon Thomson upon the joys of office. Disraeli was not to enjoy a long retirement, as he died within a year. When he was dying, he was asked whether he would welcome a visit from the Queen. Declining the great honour, he said: 'She would only ask me to take a message to Albert.' Gladstone would not go to his funeral, pleading pressure of work. He did say,

however, 'May the Almighty be near his pillow.' But he could not resist confiding his true feeling in his diary: 'As he lived, so he died – all display without reality or genuineness.'

At a dinner after Disraeli's death, Gladstone asked his hostess whether it was true that Dizzy took primroses to the Queen at Windsor. When he was told that this was correct, Gladstone expressed his surprise, saying: 'I'd have thought that the gorgeous lily was more to his taste.'

GORDON AND KHARTOUM, 1885

*G*ordon had been sent to Egypt to *disengage from the Sudan. He did exactly the reverse. He decided to destroy the Sudanese rebel leader, generally known as the Mahdi. Early in 1885, Gordon and his forces were massacred at Khartoum. A few days after the news had reached London, Gladstone went to the Criterion Theatre. He defended this incredibly insensitive act by pointing out that by then Gordon's death had still not been finally confirmed. One music-hall song reversed the initials GOM – 'the Grand Old Man', which his followers had given him – to MOG – 'Murderer of Gordon'.*

Four months later the Government's will to continue collapsed. The artist here is G. Bridgman.

KHARTOUM & CRITERION

Two years later, the charismatic General Gordon was sent to the Sudan to deal with a Holy War that had been raised by a local leader, known as the Mahdi, against the infidel British. Gordon far exceeded his orders and was eventually besieged in Khartoum. Gladstone so delayed sending a relief army that it reached the city two days after it had fallen and Gordon had been killed. All hell broke loose in England. Gladstone was hissed and jeered as he left No. 10; the Queen blamed him in an unciphered telegram, which was leaked.

It was, however, Irish politics that came to dominate British politics. The Irish Nationalist Party came into existence in the 1870s and soon controlled most of the Irish seats at Westminster. Its main policy was to demand House Rule, with a separate Parliament sitting in Dublin. It used tactics in the House of Commons to disrupt business, which bedevilled Parliament. A different body, the Land League, was established to bring relief to many of the peasants in Ireland who were suffering from near famine.

Charles Stewart Parnell became leader of both the Nationalist Party and the Land League. His position was truly paradoxical, for he was a Protestant landowner who came to be the hero of Catholic peasants. He had a cold and distant manner – it was said of him that he had all the qualities of a poker except its warmth – but underneath that surface there was real passion.

Gladstone's first reaction to the troubles was to introduce a Land Act to improve the lot of the Irish peasants. But he was forced to introduce a policy of coercion following the murder of the Chief Secretary of Ireland,

THE WEEKLY FREEMAN, 1885

This Irish cartoon comments on the immense opportunities that the 1885 General Election results seemed to present to Parnell and the Irish Nationalists.

Parnell has dealt the cards. Prime Minister Salisbury is encouraged by Lord Randolph Churchill to bid for the Irish vote, while Gladstone discusses the position gloomily with Joseph Chamberlain. At the 1885 General Election, Parnell had urged

Irish voters to support the Conservatives. Very soon after this cartoon appeared, the Conservatives repudiated their loose alliance with the Irish, while Gladstone announced his own conversion to Home Rule. Parnell's rash support for the Conservatives damaged the prospects for Home Rule in two ways. It reduced the number of Liberals in the House of Commons; and it made some Liberals so angry with the Irish that they were disposed to support the Liberal Unionist revolt against Gladstone.

THE GREAT BALLOT BOXING MATCH, 1885

*U*ntil 1918, General Elections *normally lasted for several weeks. This cartoon by J. Gordon Thomson appeared while the 1885 Election was still in progress. Early results had suggested that the Liberals would regain control from the Conservatives. The Prime Minister Salisbury is dazed; his second, Lord Randolph Churchill, tries to encourage him. Gladstone wears a kilt because of his association with Midlothian and prepares for the knock-out blow.*

IN SUSPENSE, OR HOW LONG WILL IT HOLD?, 1886

*I*n June 1886 Gladstone's Irish Home *Rule Bill was defeated by ninety-three of the Chamberlain Liberals voting with the Tories. Gladstone, at the age of seventy-seven, had made five speeches on the Bill. In his final wind-up speech, he said, 'Ireland stands at your bar, expectant, hopeful, almost supplicant . . . she asks a blessed oblivion of the past and in that oblivion our interest is even deeper than hers.' Gladstone dissolved Parliament. The Liberals were routed and Salisbury became Prime Minister.*

Tom Merry, whose real name was William Mecham, was a Tory, the scourge of Gladstone and the Liberals. Each week he drew large coloured lithographs for the St Stephen's Review. *Vivid and striking, they were published as separate pictures, rather like the 18th-Century prints.*

THE TOBOGGAN SLIDE, 1891

The politicians in the snow are in fact Irish MPs who are alarmed that Gladstone's passionate commitment to Home Rule was leading to a spill. Cartoon by Tom Merry.

Lord Frederick Cavendish, in Phoenix Park, Dublin in 1882. Cavendish was a distant relation to the Prime Minister and Gladstone was deeply moved by his death; he had an almost paternal affection for him.

Gladstone had said, as early as 1868, that his mission was to pacify Ireland. During the early 1880s he moved slowly but inexorably towards accepting Home Rule. The Conservatives had no such doubts. Their most popular orator was Lord Randolph Churchill, the father of Winston, who urged the Conservative Party 'to play the orange card'. This meant total opposition to Home Rule, and particularly a refusal to allow the Protestants in the North to be subject to a Government in Dublin. Home Rule was Rome Rule. Churchill had a Liberal counterpart in Joseph Chamberlain, a rich screw manufacturer who had risen through local politics in Birmingham to a commanding position in the Liberal Party. He joined the Cabinet in 1880 as one of its most radical members. Like Charles James Fox a century earlier, Chamberlain was never to become Prime Minister, but he was to have a profound effect upon the politics of his time. Within the space of twenty-five years, he divided and broke first the Liberal Party and then the Conservative Party.

In 1885 Gladstone was defeated in the House of Commons and resigned, but it was not possible to hold the customary General Election. In 1884 the Third Reform Act enfranchised many new voters; the electoral procedures had not been fully implemented and so there were no up-to-date registers. The Liberals agreed to allow Salisbury to form an administration until a General Election could be held. This was dubbed by Chamberlain, 'The Government of Caretakers'. The General Election at the end of 1885 left the Liberals as still the largest party, but they were balanced by the Conservatives and the Irish Nationalists taken together. After a defeat in the House of Commons, Salisbury resigned and Gladstone assumed office again, announcing his conversion to Home Rule.

WILL THEY WORK?, 1892

*S*ir William Harcourt, drawn here as *a gillie, was the Chancellor of the Exchequer. He holds four hounds in leash – the Labour Party, the Radicals, the Nationalists and the Parnellites. Rosebery, reluctantly the Foreign Secretary, is wondering 'What sort of "bag" he'll make over those dogs?' Gladstone was Prime Minister again in*

1892, but he depended upon the votes of the Irish. He got their support for Home Rule, but had long lost the support of the Liberal Unionists.

As Tenniel used a pencil, his cartoons are very softly drawn. He then traced them on to a woodblock where his engraver, Swain, would try to capture the fineness, but inevitably they appeared in Punch *with much darker lines.*

THE GRAND OLD MAN, 1893

Harry Furniss was the first cartoonist to sit and draw in the Gallery of the House of Commons. His sketches were rapid, exciting and alive. Here he portrays the old Gladstone in full flood. The young Winston Churchill saw Gladstone introduce the Second Home Rule Bill from the Strangers' Gallery in the House of Commons. He said of this performance, 'The Grand Old Man looked like a great white eagle, at once fierce and splendid.'

Gladstone soon introduced the first Home Rule Bill to establish two separate Parliaments for Great Britain and Ireland. This was defeated on the Second Reading by 30 votes. Although most of the Liberals and Irish Nationalists voted for it, over 90 Liberal MPs, including the 'Whig' Hartington and the 'Radical' Joseph Chamberlain, voted against it. This group became known as the Liberal Unionists.

The Liberal Party was divided, but the Conservatives were not. Salisbury laid down the doctrine, 'Ireland must be kept, like India, at all hazards, by permission if possible, if not by force.' Another General Election in 1886 gave Salisbury a working majority. In that election Churchill made the memorable description of Gladstone as 'an old man in a hurry'. The divisions in the Liberal Party allowed the Conservatives to be in office for most of the next twenty years.

Salisbury was to be Prime Minister for 14 years – the third longest period of any Prime Minister. He got a fourth class degree, an achievement later equalled by Alec Douglas-Home. He was left so short of money by his father that he turned to journalism, writing some masterly expositions on the nature of Conservatism for the *Political Quarterly*. He believed that the country was governed best if it was governed least. For most of the time he combined the post of Prime Minister and Foreign Secretary, ensuring that Britain came top in the scramble for Africa. But he was essentially a negotiator who sought victories through diplomacy – he was not a warmonger.

Most cartoons of Salisbury show him as a very fat, rather somnolent but good-natured man. He did not have much time for democracy, warning against 'placing a great Empire under the absolute control of the

THE TROUBLED MIND, 1894

*R*osebery was chosen by Victoria; he would not have been Gladstone's recommendation, while neither the Liberal Cabinet nor the MPs were consulted. He was at dagger's drawn with his Chancellor of the Exchequer, Sir William Harcourt, and later he wrote to Gladstone, 'The firm of Rosebery and Harcourt was a fraud upon the public.'

This cartoon by Harry Furniss shows not only the political troubles that beset him, but also his nervous and troubled state of mind. The strain of office intensified his natural insomnia and he cracked up.

poorest classes in the towns'. Later he appointed his nephew, Arthur Balfour, a future Prime Minister, as the Irish Secretary. As the Prime Minister's first name was Robert, this gave new meaning to the expression, 'Bob's your Uncle'.

Salisbury's commanding position as Prime Minister was never really challenged. In 1886 he got shot of Lord Randolph Churchill, the darling of the Conservatives in the constituencies. As Chancellor of the Exchequer, Churchill offered his resignation over a dispute on the Budget, believing that Salisbury would never accept it. The Prime Minister did just that, relieved that the most colourful and charismatic member of his Government had committed political suicide. Salisbury appointed the Liberal Unionist, Goschen, in his place. This led Churchill to comment ruefully, 'I forgot Goschen.'

ROSEBERY, 1905

*T*his later caricature of Rosebery by Max Beerbohm reminded the public that Rosebery was very much still around, but his reputation was much higher than his achievement. He was a gifted speaker whom many had thought would be a natural successor to Gladstone, in spite of the fact that his instincts were Conservative rather than Radical. Churchill's comment was shrewd and accurate: 'At first, they said, "He will come." Then for years, "If only he would come." And finally, long after he had renounced politics forever, "If only he would come back."'

In the General Election of 1892 the Liberals became the largest party – though they lacked an overall majority. So Gladstone, at the age of 82, became Prime Minister for the fourth time. His Government was dominated by Ireland. Gladstone drew up the second Home Rule Bill and argued for it passionately clause by clause in the House of Commons. The Bill passed through the Commons, but was rejected by the Lords by a margin of 10–1. A few months later Gladstone resigned and was replaced by the Earl of Rosebery, who was one of the relatively few Whigs who had stayed loyal to the Grand Old Man. At his last Cabinet, several members broke down and wept, to Gladstone's disgust. He dismissed it with contempt as the 'Blubbering Cabinet'.

Rosebery was immensely rich, inheriting one fortune and marrying another. His short administration was racked with dissension, just as he was racked with insomnia, which he tried to cure by driving around London during the night in his primrose-coloured carriage. The colour was chosen because Rosebery's family name was Primrose. Nonconformist Liberals were shocked when his horses, Ladas in 1894 and Sir Visto in 1895, won the Derby.

Rosebery had a wretched time and succumbed to a nervous breakdown. At the age of 47 he left office, never to return. Over the next twenty years he kept reappearing in public affairs, usually embarrassing his former friends.

12 · The End of the Old Order

PRIME MINISTERS
June 1895: 3rd Marquess of Salisbury (3rd Ministry)
July 1902: Arthur Balfour (later Earl Balfour)
December 1905: Sir Henry Campbell-Bannerman
April 1908–December 1916: Herbert Henry Asquith (later first
Earl of Oxford & Asquith)

CHURCHILL described Rosebery's Government as 'a bleak, precarious, wasting inheritance'. In June 1895, when it was defeated on a minor matter in a thin House, Rosebery resigned. Lord Salisbury formed a Government and invited the Liberal Unionists, including Joseph Chamberlain, to join his Cabinet. So when he went to the country it was as a Conservative/Liberal Unionist alliance. Salisbury held the premiership rather like a Platonic Guardian, out of a sense of public duty rather than with an eagerness for power. If we discount a single day in 1963, he was the last Peer to be Prime Minister.

Chamberlain was appointed Colonial Secretary – the post he wanted, although it was a relatively junior one. Salisbury was ageing and the driving force of the Government was Chamberlain, who 'made the political weather'. These two men were poles apart, both as people and as politicians. Salisbury was the grandee, carelessly dressed, slow to act and imbued with Christian cynicism; Chamberlain was the man of the new age, immaculately turned out with a monocle and orchid, rattling with radical ideas and looking upon the colonies with a businessman's eyes as 'undeveloped estates'.

A.J. BALFOUR, 1903

The witty and acerbic cartoons of Max Beerbohm, the gifted essayist and theatre critic, were in direct contrast to the pompous portrayals in Punch. Balfour was a wilting question mark, Lloyd George a little twister, Asquith lifeless, Baldwin thoughtless and Bonar Law senseless. He used an incredible economy of line and ironic captions. His cartoons are rarely about specific political events, they delineate character: in every sense of the word, Max was incomparable.

130

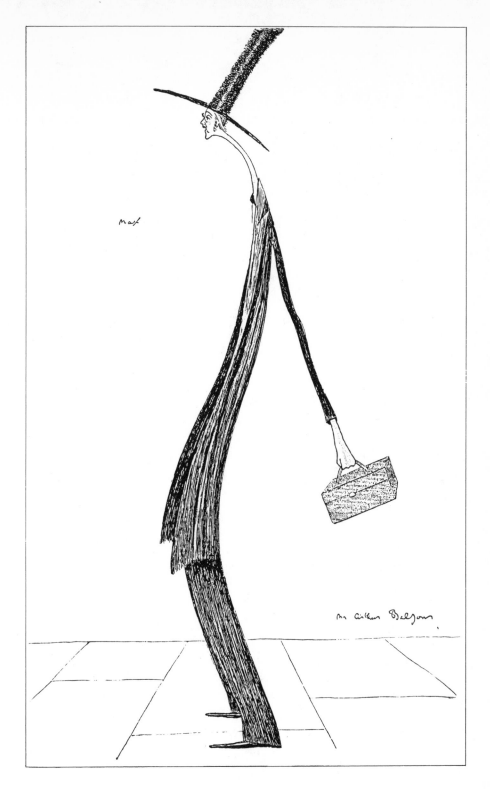

Max

Mr Arthur Balfour

POLITICAL SLIMNESS, 1900

*I*n 1900, Lord Roberts reversed the defeats suffered by the British Army. He swept the Boers before him, relieving Kimberley, Ladysmith and, in May, Mafeking. This was greeted in Britain with jubilant rejoicing and spontaneous street parties. Chamberlain persuaded Salisbury to call an election two years before it was due. The Conservatives had been losing by-elections and the chance of wrapping the Government in the Union Jack could not be resisted. But in this Khaki Election they gained only three seats overall.

This cartoon was drawn by Francis Carruthers Gould. He was a committed Liberal and, following the Liberal landslide of 1906, he was knighted. His portrait hangs alongside the other Liberal heroes in the National Liberal Club. He had joined the Pall Mall Gazette in 1888 and was the first staff caricaturist on a daily newspaper. His drawings, on the whole, are rather kindly.

The Government became dominated by South Africa. The Boers, who had established an independent state in the Transvaal, which had vast reserves of diamonds and gold, were an awkward nuisance to the great Imperial vision shared by Chamberlain and Cecil Rhodes, the wealthy Prime Minister of Cape Colony. Rhodes wanted a Cape to Cairo railway running through lands that were either British colonies or under British control. Rhodes once remarked, 'To be an Englishman was to have won the first prize in the lottery of life.'

ALICE HAS TEA AT THE HOTEL CECIL, 1900

Gould could not resist attacking the Tories again. Salisbury is the Dormouse, Balfour the March Hare, Chamberlain the Mad Hatter. This was an illustration to the satirical booklet, The Westminster Alice, by the master of irony, Saki. It is a tribute to Tenniel, who is here remembered not for his political cartoons but for his illustrations for Alice in Wonderland. These are so memorable that they continue to inspire cartoons today.

DIFFICULT STEERING, 1901

The motor car was a recent invention: Salisbury, who liked new-fangled things, is driven past obstacles by Balfour. From the late 18th Century, the offices of Prime Minister and First Lord of the Treasury had nearly always for practical purposes been the same thing. Salisbury's Government of 1895–1902 was the last occasion on which they were separate. Balfour was the First Lord of the Treasury, who spoke for the Government in the House of Commons, and therefore had an authority not much less than that of the Prime Minister, who sat in the Lords. In that sense, Balfour's succession after Salisbury's resignation in 1902 was almost automatic.

Linley Sambourne was the main political cartoonist for Punch from 1901 to 1910. He liked to take photographs of people in the pose of politicians, whom he then drew as a basis for his heavily hatched cartoons.

The End of the Old Order 133

The British High Commissioner in South Africa, Sir Alfred Milner, intensified the pressure on the Boers and this led to the outbreak of war in October 1899. Britain was astonished by a series of humiliating defeats at the hands of the Boer farmers, who were expert horsemen and expert shots. But in 1900 the initiative was regained by British forces led by Lord Roberts, widely known as 'Bobs'.

In September 1900, the Conservatives had called the famous Khaki Election, which consolidated their majority, but did not increase it. The Liberals were divided over the War. Rosebery and Asquith generally supported the war, but others, like the rising young Welsh Liberal MP, David Lloyd George, opposed it. Like most wars, the Boer War revealed appalling incompetence. Britain was totally isolated and it was a great diversion from the struggle for power that was beginning to emerge in Europe. The war, however, drifted on for a further bitter 18 months.

FOR LOOK AT MR CHAMBERLAIN, 1903

In 1903 Chamberlain, in a speech at Birmingham, his political base, launched his campaign for Imperial preference, or 'Tariff Reform', as he called it. He wanted to turn the Empire into a vast trading entity, with Free Trade between the mother country and the colonies, but protected against outsiders by high tariff walls. This split the Conservative Party. Chamberlain's campaign was a Godsend to the Liberals who, up to that time, had shown every sign themselves of breaking up. They found a new unity in supporting Free Trade.

This cartoon was a postcard, used in the debates held right across the country.

HANDS CUT OFF, 1903

Gould's up-dating of a favourite children's book, Struwelpeter. It was a collection of rather heartless stories, today almost forgotten. The cruelty of Joe cutting off Balfour's hands was meant to raise a chuckle!

134 *The End of the Old Order*

BLONDIN, 1906

Sir Henry Campbell-Bannerman became the Leader of the Liberal MPs in 1899. He was a compromise, for there were deep splits in the Party; he was chosen to keep the balance. Here he is depicted by Gould as the famous acrobat, Charles Blondin, who was renowned for keeping his balance on a tightrope, once crossing the Niagara Falls. The balls at the end of the balancing rod carry the faces of Lord Rosebery on the 'right' and John Morley on the 'left'.

At the end of the war in 1902, Salisbury, who was in clear physical decline, resigned and was succeeded by Arthur Balfour. Balfour had been in the House since 1874, but typically he had waited two years before making his maiden speech. At Cambridge he was known as 'Pretty Fanny', preferring the company of an aesthetic group of like-minded people, 'The Souls'. His first book was entitled, *A Defence of Philosophic Doubt*, his manner was diffident and effete. He summed up his political philosophy when he said, 'The first duty of a politician is to remain in office.'

Balfour was frustrated in this aim by Joseph Chamberlain's campaign for Tariff Reform, which was launched in 1903 as an attempt to revive protectionism, and which split the Tory Party. Balfour tried to sit on the fence in this great fiscal controversy and ended up by alienating the enthusiasts on both sides. In December 1905, thinking the Liberals might be divided on another matter, he resigned. Nevertheless, Balfour kept popping up in various positions in various governments. As Foreign Secretary in 1917, he issued the famous Balfour Declaration which proposed the establishment of Palestine as a home for the Jews. Churchill said of him, 'He was like a powerful cat, walking delicately and unsoiled across a rather muddy street.'

It was Sir Henry Campbell-Bannerman who formed a Liberal Government, and then went to the country. The General Election of 1906 was a Liberal landslide. Balfour lost his seat and the Liberals had a majority of 356. The 69-year-old Campbell-Bannerman was a good-humoured Scot whose wealth came from his family drapery business. He had

The End of the Old Order 135

Bernard Partridge

A BIT OF A BREEZE, 1907

*T*he Prime Minister, Campbell-
Bannerman, witnesses a dispute
between two young working-class
women who represent the two different
parts of the Labour movement. Men of
working-class origin had sat in the
House of Commons since 1874.
Taking the Liberal Whip, they were
commonly called 'Lib-Labs'. The
forerunner of the Labour Party, the
Labour Representation Committee
(LRC), was formed in 1900. It insisted
on LRC MPs being separate from the
older political parties.
  In the 1906 Election, 25 Lib/Labs
were returned and 29 LRC MPs. After
this Election, the LRC MPs declared
themselves 'The Labour Party', to the
hostility of the Lib-Labs. C-B was
witnessing the formation of a Party
that was eventually to replace his own.

become the Liberal leader in 1899 almost by default, but he went on to
form one of the most distinguished Governments of the century, which
included Asquith, Lloyd George and Grey, as well as Churchill, who was
in a junior post. Cartoons depict 'C-B' as a genial and kindly figure.

'C-B' liked Europe, but had never visited the USA or India or any
other part of the Empire. With his ailing wife he spent six weeks of each
year taking the waters at Marienbad. When events in London became too
oppressive he would take the train to Dover, cross to Calais and have a
good lunch at the Gare Maritime. In 1908, however, he became seriously
ill and resigned. He actually died at No. 10 – the only 20th-Century Prime
Minister to do so.

The new Prime Minister, Asquith, had to deal with a series of crises –
political, social, military and constitutional – for the period was one of
quite exceptional turbulence. Asquith's temperament, summed up in the
phrase 'Wait and see', and his rather noble, patrician manner – although
he was the product of a professional middle-class family – helped to steer
the country though these difficulties. He was capable of being decisive,
and Campbell-Bannerman had nicknamed him, 'The Sledgehammer'.

The Tory majority in the House of Lords was close to 400 and Balfour used it to block or amend several Bills on Education, Land Reform and Licensing, causing Lloyd George to dub the Lords, 'Mr Balfour's poodle'. The Lords foolishly abandoned the old tradition that they should not interfere with money Bills and rejected Lloyd George's radical Budget of 1909. This forced the General Election of January 1910.

The Liberals and the Conservatives were almost equally balanced, but, with Labour and Irish Nationalist support, the Budget was passed. Asquith then proposed to limit the delaying powers of the House of Lords; but suddenly the king, Edward VII, died. A Constitutional Conference was called to try to work out a compromise and avoid facing George V with a great crisis. But the Lords again rejected the Government's proposals and another General Election was held in December. Lloyd George was in fine fettle: 'An aristocracy is like cheese: the older it is, the higher it becomes.'

The result was virtually unchanged. Asquith then played his trump card by persuading the King that, if necessary, enough Liberal Peers were to be created to carry the measure through the House of Lords. The Tories

MR LLOYD GEORGE AND THE BUDGET, 1909

*T*he *new Chancellor of the Exchequer, Lloyd George, is being buzzed by the bee, 'Deficit'. He was about to bring in his famous Budget, which increased Income Tax and Death Duties, and introduced new Land Taxes, as well as a Super Tax. These were needed to pay for more ships for the Navy and for the old age pensions, which Lloyd George had introduced in 1908. By voting down this Budget, the House of Lords precipitated the Peers versus the People crisis of 1909–11.*

This cartoon was drawn by a little-known cartoonist in Plymouth, G.F. Welsford. He produced a book on the Liberal Cabinet, parodying Edward Lear's Nonsense Rhymes.

were fed up with Balfour's leadership and a movement, 'BMG' – 'Balfour Must Go' – led to him being replaced by Bonar Law, a Glasgow iron merchant who was a disciple of Joseph Chamberlain.

The next three years, leading up to the First World War, were feverish and violent, leaving Britain convulsed by large strikes, by the violence of the women's suffrage movement and by the threat of renewed violence over Irish Home Rule. In 1912, Asquith introduced a new Home Rule Bill, similar to the one in 1893.

MR ASQUITH, YOU'RE A TRAITOR!, 1911

*A*squith, supported by George V *and John Bull, is attacked by an angry Tory Peer for his handling of the constitutional crisis of 1909–11. After two General Elections in 1910 and a refusal by the House of Lords to accept measures of reform, Asquith told the Conservatives in July 1911 that if the Lords rejected the Government's proposals, then George V would create enough new Liberal Peers to sweep away the Conservative*

majority in the Upper House. This split the Tories into the Hedgers, who were prepared to accept that the game was up, and the Ditchers, who were prepared to die in the last ditch. The Government won and introduced a Parliament Bill which stripped the Lords of their right to interfere with money Bills, as well as reducing their power of delay on other Bills. In 1948, the Lords' power of veto was reduced even further. After this it would be virtually impossible for any future Prime Minister to lead a Government from the Upper House.

THE SUCCESSION, 1911

*T*his cartoon appeared in the Daily
Mail. *Beerbohm emphasizes, not
for the first time, the untrustworthiness
of Lloyd George and Churchill.
Churchill is saying to Lloyd George,
'Come, suppose we toss for it, Davey?'
To which Lloyd George replies, 'Ah
but, Winsie, would either of us abide
by the result?'*

BALFOUR AND THE
POLICEMAN, 1911

*B*eerbohm captures Balfour's
*lackadaisical approach to the daily
grind of opposition politics – pointing
to the House of Commons, he is asking
the policeman what happens there. He
was not cut out for leading the
Opposition against one of the greatest
debaters of this century, Lloyd George,
who once said that after Balfour had
left the room all that remained was the
scent on a handkerchief.*

Asquith had not handled these crises well and, in particular, had not
contained the belligerence of Churchill. He was too casual. During
Cabinet meetings he wrote long, affectionate letters to a 21-year-old girl,
Venetia Stanley, and his heavy drinking earned him the nickname,
'Squiffy'. All these domestic difficulties were, however, submerged in the
greater crisis of the 1914 War.

Asquith was not cut out to be a war leader. In 1915 a coalition government was formed and a press campaign was started to replace Asquith

The End of the Old Order 139

DELIVERING THE GOODS, 1915

*T*here was a shortage of shells and other armaments. In 1915, Lloyd George asked to be Minister for Munitions, in wartime a more important position than that of Chancellor of the Exchequer. In 1914 less than a million shells were produced, in 1915 23 million, by 1916 128 million. Between 1915 and 1916 the production of guns was increased sixfold. Kitchener thought that each battalion needed four machine guns. Lloyd George said, 'Take Kitchener's

figure. Square it. Multiply by two. Then double again for good luck.' This is what Lloyd George was really best at – getting things done, galvanzing people into action. He had little influence upon the strategy of the war; but, then, who did? A peacetime economy was transformed in record time. Twenty thousand small factories supplied the forces and many made fortunes out of the war.

This cartoon was by Leonard Raven Hill, who drew cartoons in Punch that did not surprise, or create resentment. His social cartoons went deeper.

by Lloyd George. At the end of 1916, following a short, sharp political crisis, Asquith was driven to resign. 'Wait and see' was replaced by 'Push and go'. As time went went on, Asquith and Lloyd George became alienated. Asquith's second wife, Margot Tennant, said of Lloyd George, 'He cannot see a belt without hitting below it.'

The Liberal Party, which had started with a huge majority in 1906, had lost its authority and has not formed a Government since.

MUDDLES, 1916

*A*squith's temperament was not suited to being a war leader. He also run out of luck. The year 1916 was calamitous – the Dardenelles campaign had collapsed; there was rebellion in Ireland in Easter week; he had had to introduce compulsory military service with great reluctance; and the British offensive under Haig, on the Somme in August, resulted in the worst losses any British Army had ever suffered.

Some Conservatives, led by the Ulster leader, Carson, started the long process of intrigue that led to Asquith's resignation in December 1916. As Bonar Law could not form a Government, George V asked Lloyd George to do so. Lloyd George was the first man of the people to become Prime Minister or, as he put it himself, he was the first, with the exception of Disraeli, 'who had not passed through the staff college of the old universities'.

This cartoon was drawn by Edward Tennyson Reed, the only cartoonist of note who was the son of an MP. His cartoons appeared in Punch *and* The Sketch. *He was good humoured and drew very good facial likenesses. He used the old Victorian trick of taking a popular and well-recognized painting, in this case* Bubbles *by Millais, which Pears Soap had bought to use as an advertisement.*

13 · Lloyd George and Liberal Decline

PRIME MINISTERS
December 1916: David Lloyd George
October 1922: Andrew Bonar Law. *April 1923:* Stanley Baldwin
January 1924–November 1924: Ramsay MacDonald

LLOYD GEORGE immediately created a small War Cabinet of five ministers to conduct the war, and, for the first time, Cabinet minutes were circulated. He was not able to control the generals, particularly Haig, who could count on support from the King and the Tories. But he did persuade the Navy to reduce losses by using convoys. Above all, Lloyd George galvanized the 'Nation in Arms'.

It was one of the great ironies of history that the radical Welsh lawyer, who had been a pacifist in the Boer War, was now sustained by the Tory Party as a war leader. The Liberal Party was gradually split by the personalities of Asquith and Lloyd George. The split was confirmed in an important parliamentary vote in May 1918 when 98 Liberal MPs supported Asquith and only 71 Lloyd George, but the Unionists backed him to the hilt. The Liberal Party never fully recovered.

In December 1918, after the Armistice, Lloyd George held an election in which he campaigned for a coalition led by himself and Bonar Law. This was the famous 'Coupon Election', so-called because coalition candidates were blessed with a letter of support from both leaders, nicknamed 'the coupon'. For the first time, a mass electorate participated. In 1910 there were 8 million voters and in 1918 there were 22 million. Votes were given to women over the age of 30 – the munitions workers in the war had won what the suffragettes before the war had failed to achieve. It was a dirty campaign. Lloyd George played the nationalist card; Asquith lost his seat.

The MPs who supported the coalition government from 1918 to 1922 were described later by Stanley Baldwin as 'hard-faced men who looked as though they had done well out of the War'. The Cabinet was full of flamboyant characters – 'Birds of paradise' in Lord Beaverbrook's phrase – men like Churchill, Curzon and F.E. Smith. The only thing that held them together was a love of power.

INDECENT HASTE, 1918

A General Election was overdue by three years. Lloyd George wanted the continuation of a National Coalition. He offered Asquith the Lord Chancellorship and the Labour Party a place. George Bernard Shaw, three days after the Armistice, said to a Labour Conference, 'Go back to Lloyd George and say: "Nothing Doing".'

This cartoon appeared in November in the newspaper that supported Labour, the Herald. Lloyd George and Bonar Law agreed to support coalition candidates and there was an electoral pact whereby such approved candidates did not stand against each other. The issue of the Coupon Election was Lloyd George – 'The Man Who Won The War'. All men above the age of 21, including soldiers of course, received the vote, even if they were not householders. Lloyd George won a massive majority and the Labour Leader, Ramsay MacDonald, was punished for his pacificism by losing his seat.

Indecent Haste was drawn by the Australian socialist, Will Dyson, who had settled in London in 1909. He was the first cartoonist whose sympathies were totally for the working class: here the suffering soldier, not the well-dressed politician, wins the war. His drawings are vivid and he reintroduced vigour and even violence in cartooning. He was one of the major cartoonists of the early 20th Century, though the quality of his work varied enormously.

THE NEW HEROIC TENOR IN ENGLAND, 1916

*T*his was how Lloyd George was
* seen in the German satirical
magazine,* Kladderadatsch. *The King,
George V, recognizes that Lloyd
George will sing 'Rule Britannia' better
than Asquith. German cartoons of the
period ascribed to the King a greater
influence over events than he actually
possessed.*

It was Lloyd George's heyday. Bonar Law commented, 'Lloyd George can be Prime Minister for life if he wants.' He believed he could do almost anything and he ran the country with a team in Downing Street dubbed the 'Garden Suburb'. He created his own war chest through the sale of honours. He had a well-earned reputation as a womanizer but his amorous adventures were not recorded in any cartoon. Frances Stephenson, his secretary at No. 10, became his mistress and later his wife.

In the early 1920s unemployment in 'the land fit for heroes to live in' rose to over 20 per cent. Conservative MPs met at the Carlton Club and, disregarding the advice of their own Party leaders, decided that they would no longer sustain the Coalition Government. They were particularly influenced by a speech from Stanley Baldwin, who said of Lloyd George, 'A dynamic force is a terrible thing.' Baldwin, who had become President of the Board of Trade in 1921, had entered politics late after a successful career as a Midlands industrialist. The Coalition broke up and Lloyd George resigned.

Lloyd George's successor was Andrew Bonar Law. Since most of the Conservative leaders refused to serve under him, his Government was dubbed, 'the Government of the Second XI'. But Bonar Law held an election and won a majority of 200 over the Labour Party, which then emerged as the leading opposition party for the first time.

Bonar Law had managed to hold the Conservative Party together by leading it from the right of centre. He had supported Protection and Ulster, describing his role as Leader of the Conservative Party in these memorable words, 'I must follow them, I am their Leader.' He was to be Prime Minister for only 209 days, for he contracted an incurable throat cancer. At his funeral in Westminster Abbey, Asquith, who had always looked down upon Bonar Law, said: 'It is not inappropriate that we have buried the Unknown Prime Minister beside the Unknown Soldier.'

As Bonar Law was virtually speechless and barely capable of writing because of his illness, he did not recommend a successor to George V. Many thought that the King would choose the most experienced Conservative politician, George, Marquis of Curzon. He was not the most popular of Conservative leaders, but being in the House of Lords was the crucial disadvantage, and so he entered the ranks of those who have just missed being Prime Minister.

Instead, George V called the Chancellor of the Exchequer, Stanley Baldwin. His rise had been spectacularly fast. In 1916, Baldwin had been appointed Parliamentary Private Secretary – not even on the payroll – to Bonar Law. Within six years he found himself in No. 10. His Government lasted only 8 months because Baldwin announced his support for Protection and decided to hold an election in December on the old issue

THE ARGUMENT, 1921

*D*avid Low, a New Zealander, *created the image of the Coalition Government as a two-headed donkey ridden by Lloyd George – such a strong and accurate portrayal that it probably helped towards the Coalition's defeat.*

Low created a series of striking images that had considerable political influence from the 1920s through to the 1950s and is considered by many to be the finest cartoonist of the 20th Century. His standing was so high that when he worked for The Guardian, *towards the end of his life, his salary was greater than that of the Managing Director. He started by drawing for the* Star *and then moved to the* Evening Standard, *where Beaverbrook gave him complete freedom to lash whomsoever he wanted – usually the Tories.*

THE SALE OF HONOURS, 1922

*D*uring the Coalition, Honours were sold on a large scale. Some of the money went to Lloyd George's own political fund, which was quite separate from that of the Liberal Party. Knighthoods cost £10,000; baronetcies £40,000; peerages went for over £100,000. The agent Lloyd George used was Maundy Gregory, who later went to jail.

Lloyd George told J.C. Davidson of the Conservative Party: 'You and I know that the sale of honours is the cleanest way of raising money for a political party. The worst of it is that you can't defend it in public.' The sales later led to the Prevention of Abuses Act, 1925.

INTO THE LIMELIGHT, 1922

*I*n the Election of 1922 the Labour Party became the largest opposition party. This was Ramsay MacDonald's finest hour. He had had a chequered career in the Labour Party. He was its Chairman in 1914 when, as a pacifist, he was displaced by Arthur Henderson, who later became the first Labour Minister to serve in a Cabinet in the wartime coalitions. MacDonald lost his seat in 1918 and only managed to return to the House in 1922. At that election Henderson himself lost his seat. MacDonald was thus very lucky to become leader of the Labour Party again. Within 18 months he was himself in No. 10 as the first Labour Prime Minister. This cartoon was by Bernard Partridge, who was Punch's chief cartoonist from 1910 until 1945.

MARK MY FOOTSTEPS, GOOD MY PAGE, 1923

*Cartoonists have revelled in
depicting the succession of a
powerful Prime Minister by a lesser
figure – Addington after Pitt, Eden
after Churchill, John Major after
Margaret Thatcher and, in this cartoon
by Strube, Bonar Law after Lloyd
George.*

*Sidney 'George' Strube drew for the
Daily Express from 1918 to 1948. His
most famous creation was 'The Little
Man', with his umbrella, bow-tie and
bowler hat, with whom the reader was
asked to identify. His cartoons became
very popular and, like Low, he earned
much from them.*

of Free Trade or Protection. It was a mistake that united the Liberals. The Conservatives lost 90 seats; the Labour Party, led by Ramsay MacDonald, emerged again as the leading opposition party, with 191 seats. The diehard Tories were appalled at the prospect of a Labour Government. After a Commons defeat in January 1924, Baldwin resigned.

George V acted in accordance with constitutional precedent in calling for the Leader of the Opposition, Ramsay MacDonald, to form a Government although he did not have a majority in the Commons. MacDonald was, at that time, not even a member of the Privy Council and so, before becoming Prime Minister, he had to be sworn in – the only Prime Minister in our history for whom this was necessary.

MacDonald was allowed to be Prime Minister for under a year – he was in office but not in power. In the General Election of October 1924, Labour was hit hard for being too pro-Soviet and lost 40 seats. But the real losers were the Liberals. For two years Asquith had believed that he was the puppetmaster and would somehow manipulate himself back into office. In the Election of 1924, the Liberal Party was manipulated into near oblivion.

Lloyd George and Liberal Decline 147

14 · Baldwin and Co

PRIME MINISTERS

November 1924: Stanley Baldwin (later 1st Earl Baldwin of Bewdley)
(Second Government)

June 1929: J. Ramsay MacDonald (Labour Government)
(Second Government)

August 1931: J. Ramsay MacDonald (National Government)

June 1935: Stanley Baldwin (Third Government)

May 1937–May 1940: Neville Chamberlain

STANLEY BALDWIN dominated British politics from 1923 to 1937. He had a calm, reflective manner, placidly smoking his pipe; he was essentially a conciliator, a seeker of compromise. He discovered consensus politics. His love of the English countryside and the English language inspired his most moving speeches, which encapsulated the spirit of England. Yet he had to deal with political characters who were more eloquent, populist and charismatic. It is a tribute to the tenacity of his character that Baldwin effectively checked the careers of both Lloyd George and Churchill. As a result, they both probably rather overrated his political ability. Lloyd George thought, 'He was the most formidable antagonist I ever encountered.' And Churchill said of him, 'The greatest Party manager the Conservatives ever had.'

Baldwin was at his best when practising the healing arts. Industrial unrest boiled over in the nine-day General Strike (1926) and by his handling of it he avoided violence. However, he had no ideas on how to deal with unemployment, and when he campaigned in 1929 on the slogan 'Safety First', the Conservatives were defeated. Labour became the largest party and Ramsay MacDonald was called back to No. 10.

MacDonald was 62 years old and, as Beatrice Webb, the Fabian, said, 'a magnificent substitute for a leader'. He was helped by his height and his mellifluous voice, which gave him a commanding presence. Lloyd George said that he had, 'Sufficient conscience to bother him, but not enough to keep him straight.' MacDonald had emerged from the obscure background of Lossiemouth in Scotland and was the only Prime Minister to have been born out of wedlock. He preferred foreign to domestic affairs and to his opponents he was 'the boneless wonder'. In 1930,

THE SNOW-THROWERS' ANTHEM, 1928

*T*he boys throwing snowballs at the snowman, Baldwin, are the 'Anti-Baldwin Syndicalist Press'. They shout, 'The more we throw together . . .', and Baldwin calmly responds, 'The soldier I shall be'.

Beaverbrook despised Baldwin, whom he considered diabolically cunning and innately deceitful. Beaverbrook and Rothermere ran a press campaign to persuade the Tories to ditch Baldwin as Leader. Baldwin turned to his cousin, Kipling, to write the most contemptuous dismissal: 'What the proprietorship of these papers is aiming at, is power, and power without responsibility – the prerogative of the harlot throughout the ages.'

THE TOPPER, 1926

*B*aldwin's most surprising appointment was Winston Churchill as Chancellor of the Exchequer. Churchill had had an astonishing career, starting as a Conservative and then switching to the Liberals in 1904. He became a Lloyd Georgeite during the Coalition period and fought unsuccessfully as a Liberal in the 1923 Election. In 1924 he stood as an independent in a by-election where candidates of all three parties were against him. At the General Election of the same year he described himself as a 'constitutionalist' – nobody really knew what that meant, but the local Conservative Association supported him. Baldwin brought him in as he was too dangerous to be left out. Like Disraeli, Churchill had no real understanding of figures or economic matters. He soon succumbed to the Governor of the Bank of England, who persuaded him to put Britain back on the Gold Standard in 1926. This was a disastrous mistake, which deepened the slump and increased unemployment.

THE LONG AND SHORT OF IT, 1931

*T*his demonstrates Ramsay MacDonald's dilemma during the period of the National Government. He needed the support of the Liberals, although Lloyd George could only deliver a small handful of votes – truly on the short side. Ramsay MacDonald, by working with Baldwin, kept Lloyd George in the wilderness. Lloyd George held MacDonald in contempt, saying of him in 1931, 'the ranting hero of the socialist cause squeaked with terror when he was invited to face the wrath of the financial weasels of the City. What leaders for the Revolution!'

In his cartoons of Lloyd George, Strube usually showed him accompanied by a mangoldwurzel and a pheasant. Many years before, LG had made a speech referring to pheasants, which having been bred for landlords' sport, ate, so he alleged, mangoldwurzels, which were needed for tenant farmers' cattle. There was considerable dispute among agriculturalists as to whether pheasants ever ate mangoldwurzels, but Strube never let LG forget this bit of high-flown rhetoric.

CONGRATULATIONS, MR MACDONALD, 1931

In the 1931 Election, Conservatives and their allies won 521 seats and Labour was down to a rump of about 50. Cartoon by David Low.

Harold Nicolson noted in his diary that Ramsay MacDonald had said to him, "If God were to come to me and say, 'Ramsay, would you rather be a country gentleman than a Prime Minister?', I would reply, 'Please God, a country gentleman'."

The Labour Government had no programme and few ideas. They were overwhelmed by the worldwide slump that followed the Wall Street Crash of 1929. Oswald Mosley resigned from the Cabinet when it would not accept his high-spending policies and a few years later he became the fascist leader. The Chancellor, Philip Snowden, was an austere believer in a balanced Budget and proposed a cut of 10 per cent in unemployment benefit. The trade unions, led by Ernest Bevin, would have none of it. The Cabinet split virtually evenly and the Labour Government resigned in 1931. A National Government was set up, with MacDonald still Prime Minister, and it included Tories and Liberals. The irony of this crisis was that the Labour Government fell in order to protect the pound. But within days it proved impossible to do so and Britain abandoned the Gold Standard under which sterling had been fully convertible into gold.

Ramsay MacDonald was never forgiven for what many considered to be a betrayal of his Party. He lost the leadership almost immediately; in the Election of 1931 nearly all the Labour leaders were defeated. The Labour Party was reduced to a rump of about 50 MPs. The Liberals won 33 seats and 'the Lloyd George Party' was down to just 4 – himself, his son, daughter and son-in-law.

In the National Government, Ramsay MacDonald was a figurehead, becoming progressively senile. Actual power was exercized by Baldwin. In 1935 Baldwin became Prime Minister for the third time. It was fortunate for Britain that he was Prime Minister during the Abdication Crisis in 1936, but his Government was dominated by the growing menace of Mussolini and Hitler.

A DEAD CERT, 1931

Strube shows Lloyd George's position from 1922 to 1939: not only the jockey of a dead horse, but the bookie and the punter as well.

Churchill continued to receive the Conservative Whip, but became the unofficial Leader of the Opposition. In December 1936, he delivered one of his most eloquent attacks on Baldwin's whole style: 'The Government simply cannot make up their minds, or they cannot get the Prime Minister to make up his mind . . . decided only to be undecided, resolved to be irresolute, adamant for drift, solid for fluidity, all powerful to be impotent. So we go on preparing more months and years for the locusts to eat.' Baldwin had tried dynamic leadership in 1923, when he had boldly come out for Protection, but his Government had been defeated. As far as he was concerned, never again.

Most cartoonists portrayed Baldwin as a wise and benign statesmen. But David Low savagely attacked his casual attitude to the dictators, particularly after the Election of 1936 when he had a large enough majority to have switched to a proper programme of rearmament. Baldwin's successor, Neville Chamberlain, was to fare even worse. Most of his life had been spent on domestic affairs – particularly housing and health – where he had been one of the most innovative ministers in the 1920s and 1930s. Now he was plunged into world politics and he led the policy of appeasement whose high-water mark was the Munich Agreement of 1938. Just six months after that Agreement, Hitler annexed the western part of Czechoslovakia.

For a moment, in 1938, Chamberlain was feted as one of the great peacemakers of the world. A popular song had the refrain, 'God Bless you Mr Chamberlain'. His great and eloquent opponent from the backbenches was Winston Churchill, who campaigned against appeasement. David Low shared his views. His cartoons were so effectively anti-Nazi and so pro-Churchill that Ribbentrop, the German Foreign Minister, complained about them to Halifax, the British Foreign Secretary.

AT THE POLITICAL MAGICIANS' DINNER, 1931

*T*his cartoon by George Strube
dramatically depicts the
inadequacy of all politicians and
parties when faced by the spectre of
unemployment. In the early 1930s,
there was a craze for magicians: here
all the politicians are showing off their
tricks. Lloyd George plucks a pheasant
out of MacDonald's shirt front, while
he spins a plate. Baldwin is doing a
trick with a handkerchief, while
Churchill, wearing a turban because of
his opposition to the India Bill, juggles
with a cruet. Philip Snowden does
what every Chancellor does – he
extracts money from the pockets of the
little man – while Mosley burns
Labour's policies, which are held by
the left-winger Jimmy Maxton. All are
in evening dress, but none can conjure
up work.

THE NEW SEE-SAW, 1935

*I*n 1935, Baldwin succeeded
MacDonald as Prime Minister of the
National Government. In the early
autumn Italy attacked Abyssinia and a
General Election was held. In the
campaign, Baldwin made his famous
statement, 'I give you my word, there
will be no great armaments.' Labour
did rather better than in 1931, winning
154 seats against the Government's
432. MacDonald lost his seat. The
relatively unknown Member of
Parliament for Limehouse, Major
Attlee, became Leader of the Labour
Party, and this is one of the earliest
cartoons in which he featured.

The others clinging on to the see-saw
are Jimmy Maxton, leader of the small
Independent Labour Party; Sir
Archibald Sinclair from the Liberal
Party; and Lloyd George, who is only
just holding on.

This cartoon was drawn by E.H.
Shepard, who – like Tenniel – was
more famous as a book illustrator – he
had drawn the pictures for A.A.
Milne's Winnie the Pooh books. He
was, however, a regular political
cartoonist for Punch.

When War was declared in 1939, Chamberlain invited Churchill to join the Government as First Lord of the Admiralty. Anthony Eden, who had earlier resigned as Foreign Secretary, also took office. Initially, neither the Liberal nor the Labour Parties joined the Government.

Chamberlain proved even more ineffective as a war leader than Asquith. In May 1940, a revolt of Conservative backbenchers reduced the Conservative majority to 81. At first it looked as if the appeaser Halifax, Chamberlain's Foreign Secretary, might take over, but the fact that he was a Peer fortunately made that impossible. Churchill, clearly the most suitable man for the job, then became Prime Minister. To their great credit the Labour and Liberal Parties agreed to serve under Churchill, thus ending one of the most wretched decades of British history.

YOU KNOW YOU CAN TRUST ME, 1935

A month before Mussolini's troops invaded Abyssinia in October 1935, Sir Samuel Hoare, the British Foreign Secretary, had strongly supported the League of Nations, which was meant to contain aggression. During the General Election in November both Hoare and Baldwin spoke of the importance of the League of Nations as an international conciliator and supported sanctions against Italy.

After the Election the Cabinet decided to avoid war with Mussolini at all costs. This led to the infamous 'Hoare-Laval pact', which became known in December. It proposed to give to Mussolini 60,000 square miles of Abyssinia – his aggression would have paid off. There was a public outcry and Hoare was forced to resign.

STILL HOPE, 1938
MEIN KAMPF, 1938

*C*hamberlain cherished the belief
that by meeting Hitler personally
he would be able to do a deal with him
on Czechoslovakia. At Munich they
agreed that certain Czech lands would
be ceded to Hitler. He returned to
England holding the famous piece of
paper signed by Hitler and himself
which said that Britain and Germany
would not go to war. He got a hero's
welcome and, from the window of No.
10, he made a declaration of 'Peace in
our time'. Within six months, Hitler
had seized the western parts of
Czechoslovakia. In 1939 Lloyd
George, pungent as ever, said, 'The
worst thing Neville ever did was to let
Hitler see him.' These two cartoons
appeared within three days of each
other. Illingworth in Punch took the
popular line, Low in the Evening
Standard was not taken in.

Leslie Ilingworth drew for many
magazines and newspapers, but chiefly
for Punch. Malcolm Muggeridge,

editor of Punch, said in Illingworth's
obituary that his cartoons would last
longer than Low's because they were
'satire in the grand style, rather than
mischievous quips: strategic rather
than practical'.

15 · Churchill

PRIME MINISTERS
May 1940: Winston Churchill
July 1945: Clement Attlee (later 1st Earl Attlee)
October 1951: Winston Churchill
October 1955–January 1957: Sir Anthony Eden
(later 1st Earl of Avon)

CHURCHILL sensed that he had been called by history to lead the country. On becoming Prime Minister in 1940, he felt 'as if I were walking with destiny, and that all my past life had been but a preparation for this hour and this trial'. His leadership during the Second World War has been abundantly chronicled. Constitutionally, the interesting thing was that he was not Leader of the Conservative Party when he was appointed Prime Minister, but became so soon afterwards. He presided over the War Cabinet of five ministers – two Conservatives and two Labour Members.

Churchill much preferred leading a Coalition Government. This was how the cartoonists portrayed him – the epitome of Britain. Low, and later Vicky, both from the left of the political spectrum, admired him for his opposition to fascism and appeasement. For that, they forgave him much. During the war, cartoonists blunted their cutting edge, for the very survival of the nation was at stake.

Churchill would have liked the Coalition Government to have continued, at least until the Japanese were defeated. But the Labour Party wanted an early General Election. Churchill held the Election in July 1945, hoping to capitalize upon his personal popularity and the fact that he was the greatest war leader since Chatham. The result for him was devastating – a Labour majority of 180. The memories of Conservative Governments in the inter-war years and the thorough way the Labour Party canvassed those still in uniform to propagate its ideas both told against Churchill. It was an extraordinary 'thank you' for winning the war; but it showed that voters did distinguish between a war leader, whom they admired, and the leader of a Party, with which they disagreed.

ALL BEHIND YOU, WINSTON, MAY 1940

*T*his is, perhaps, the most famous cartoon of the 20th Century. Low summarized the situation exactly – all political parties were marching in step behind Winston Churchill. Neville Chamberlain is immediately behind his successor and he remained in the Government until his health broke down later in the year. Other Conservatives are Lord Halifax, Anthony Eden, Sir Kingsley Wood and Duff Cooper. The Labour men are Clement Attlee, Arthur Greenwood, Ernest Bevin, Herbert Morrison and A.V. Alexander. The Liberal Leader, Sir Archibald Sinclair, is also there.

The three-Party coalition was exceptionally close. Even the Conservative and Labour Whips' Offices were amalgamated – there could be no greater gesture of national solidarity.

GO TO IT, JUNE 1940

*S*trube's cartoon appeared after the
evacuation of Dunkirk, when
Britain stood alone and faced the
threat of invasion. This was not only
Britain's, but Churchill's finest hour.
The cartoon was reproduced as a
poster.

BRITISH WAR AIMS?, 1941

*H*ow Churchill was cartooned in
the German press . . . He is the
aggressor. All that Germany wanted
was 'A free German life'. Goebbels
would have been proud of this one.

WELL, IF IT ISN'T WIDOW
FATIMA, WHO IS IT?, 1943

*C*hurchill flew to Casablanca for a
meeting with President Roosevelt
and General de Gaulle, but for security
reasons the whole visit was kept
completely secret. News of it was only
released on the final day.

   Osbert Lancaster virtually created
the 'pocket cartoon', which extended
for about three inches over one column
on the front page of the Daily Express.
He used the extraordinarily limited
space to great comic effect, with
caustic social comments. This is one of
the very few cartoons of his that
features a Prime Minister. By then, the
cigar had become the symbol of
Churchill, just as the cigarette holder
had become the symbol for Roosevelt.

158 *Churchill*

CIGAR SMOKE, 1943

*B*eerbohm's eloquent portrayal of Churchill's supreme self-confidence. This unpublished cartoon was found in Max Beerbohm's portfolio at the Villa Chiaro, Rapallo, after his death.

POTSDAM, 1945

*T*he Allied Leaders met in Potsdam to agree the final territorial carve-up among the victors. Stalin got Konigsberg; Poland, which had lost nearly half of her pre-1939 territory to the Soviet Union, was compensated with part of Eastern Germany. But already the Russians and the Allies were more concerned with their own interests – the Cold War had started.

A General Election was held before Potsdam, but several weeks elapsed before all the overseas service votes could be collected and counted. Churchill, as Prime Minister, therefore attended the opening sessions. While the Big Three were meeting, the news of his defeat came through. Attlee attended the final session as Prime Minister, but whether either Prime Minister was very big at Potsdam was dubious. Already, Britain's world influence was on the wane.

This was drawn by Vicky – Victor Weisz – the Hungarian socialist refugee who had settled in Britain in the 1930s. He drew first for the News Chronicle *and then for the* Daily Express. *Like Low, he admired Churchill. He was to become one of the greatest postwar political cartoonists.*

Churchill 159

"CHEER UP! THEY WILL FORGET YOU BUT THEY WILL REMEMBER ME ALWAYS"

THE LEADER OF HUMANITY

THE PARTY LEADER

TWO CHURCHILLS, 1945

Low depicts Churchill's dilemma – he appealed as a leader of the nation at war, but not as the leader of the Tory Party in peace.

Attlee assumed office with two great advantages. He had the first Labour majority in the House of Commons and he could also draw upon ministers who had had experience of office during the war. Attlee set about a programme of radical change. India was given independence; the National Health Service was established by Aneurin Bevan; and the major industries of coal, railways, steel, gas and electricity were nationalized. Mild, unassuming Attlee, frequently written off and belittled by journalists and cartoonists, was the most effective Labour Prime Minister of the century.

One of the jokes at the time was that an empty taxi arrived at No. 10 Downing Street and when the door opened, Attlee got out. But Attlee had the last word in a limerick he wrote himself:

> *Few thought he was even a starter,*
> *There were many who thought themselves smarter*
> *But he ended PM*
> *CH and OM*
> *An Earl and a Knight of the Garter.*

Foreign Affairs were left to Ernest Bevin, who treated the Foreign Office as if it were his own trade union. NATO was created; atomic weapons developed; and Berlin supported during the Russian blockade. No Tory needed to worry about the champion of British interests in the Foreign Office. However, the whole apparatus of controls and rationing, established during the war, was dismantled too slowly – there had not been much of a peace dividend. This gave a great opportunity to the Conservatives to demand an end to controls and lower taxes. In 1950, the Government had largely run out of steam and just hung on in a General Election. A year later, Attlee went to the country again.

—Disraeli and his
waistcoats

—Gladstone and his
collars

—Lord Salisbury and
his beard

—Lloyd George and
his hair and cloak

—Baldwin and his pipe

—Chamberlain and his
umbrella

—Churchill and his
hats—

BUT nothing can ever ruffle him:
—'Er, I have to . . . ahem
. . . inform this House that
the world will end tomorrow.'

PERHAPS YOU WISH ATTLEE HAD THE GLAMOUR OF . . . , 1950

*A*ttlee was the most underrated Prime Minister since the Second World War. He eschewed histrionics of any sort and would not have recognized the word 'charisma'. It was said that Churchill once commented that he was 'a modest man, with much to be modest about'.

Michael Cummings was given his first job as a cartoonist by Michael Foot of Tribune, *but from 1949 he worked for the* Daily Express. *He has drawn more Prime Ministers whom he has seen than any other living cartoonist. He was Churchill's favourite cartoonist. His sympathies are to the right of centre; while this has not prevented him sharply attacking some Tory Prime Ministers, Margaret Thatcher remained a heroine.*

The result was extraordinary. Labour got more votes than any other Party – indeed, more than it had ever polled before – but because of the vagaries of the 'first-past-the-post' system, the Conservatives had a narrow majority. Churchill, at the age of 77, returned to No. 10. Attlee remained as Leader of the Opposition for a further four years.

Churchill had not given up the role of Leader of the Opposition in 1945 and none of his former ministerial colleagues was prepared to topple him. The Conservative Party had been equipped for the postwar world by R.A. Butler at the Research Department in Central Office, but Churchill's new administration was not a very radical government. Churchill accepted the Attlee settlement and repealed virtually nothing;

FINE, BOYS – THAT'LL GET THEM, 1951

*O*ne of the Labour Party's
campaigns in 1951 was to smear
Churchill as a warmonger. The Daily
Mirror *had a famous front-page
headline: 'Whose finger is on the
trigger?' In this cartoon by Leslie
Illingworth, Manny Shinwell and
Herbert Morrison, the hard political
campaigners of the Labour Party, are
distorting Churchill's cigar into a
revolver while Attlee seems to cheer
them on. Or at the very least he
doesn't stop them.*

YES, AFTER SHUFFLING MINISTRIES, 1953

*E*den and Butler reflect ruefully
upon Churchill's outsize
personality and his capacity to
interfere in any political matters that
caught his attention. Cartoon by
Michael Cummings.

THE BRITISH PUBLIC KNOWING WHAT IT LIKES, 1954

*T*o celebrate his eightieth birthday, Parliament gave to Churchill a portrait by Graham Sutherland. Churchill loathed it and later his wife, Clemmie, burnt it. It caused a great stir at the time by its honest representation of an old, defiant man. This cartoon by Ronald Searle shows the effect of the portrait on some of Churchill's most stalwart supporters – they fume, they fulminate and they faint.

Ronald Searle is one of the great contemporary cartoonists, and this is one of his very few political cartoons.

he left industries nationalized and told his Employment Secretary to mollify the trade unions. As before, Churchill was much more interested in world affairs, particularly his relationship with the American President, Eisenhower, his old companion-in-arms.

In his second Government, the cartoonists were generally kind. He was undoubtedly a great man and a world figure; in the early 1950s, deference and respect were still shown to senior politicians. Churchill complained about cartoons that emphasized his age and hinted at senility, just as he loathed Graham Sutherland's portrait which the two Houses of Parliament gave him on his 80th birthday.

Some ministers wanted Churchill to go, but he survived their impatience and two strokes. He resigned in his 81st year, handing over to a man who had lived in his shadow for over twenty years – Anthony Eden. His comment upon his protégé was damning: 'Anthony was totally incapable of differentiating great points from small points.'

Eden's premiership will be remembered for the Suez debacle in 1956. In June, Nasser nationalized the Suez Canal and Eden was convinced that he would prevent British shipping using it. Just as he underestimated the aggressive intentions of the dictators in the 1930s, so he overestimated the aggressive intentions of Nasser twenty years later. He had decided in the thirties, eventually, to stand up to dictators and he thought he was

CHARLIE CHAPLIN, 1955

*A*ttlee resigned the leadership of the Labour Party in 1955. Like Charlie Chaplin, he fades out of the limelight. Cartoon by Leslie Illingworth.

called to do so again. He was convinced that his mission was to topple Nasser. Somewhat maniacally, he shouted over the telephone to Anthony Nutting, 'I want him destroyed, can't you understand?'

Israel agreed to invade Egypt, so that Britain and France could intervene to impose peace by occupying the Suez Canal. The invasion was bungled and there was a huge public outcry. When Eisenhower and Dulles refused to support the pound, Britain had to withdraw. Eden was rattled, worried and ill. He resigned and was succeeded by Harold Macmillan, who was the first hawk in the invasion and the first dove in the withdrawal. Suez marked the end of British illusions. It revealed the weakness of the economy; the absence of a special relationship with the United States; and the near impossibility of Britain playing the leading role in world affairs again.

THE JAW IS THE JAW OF MUSSO, BUT . . ., 1936

*T*he lesson that Eden learnt from the thirties was that it was no good appeasing dictators. You had to stand up to them. He applied that lesson to totally different circumstances in the 1950s. The artist is David Low.

O, WHITHER HAST THOU LED ME, EGYPT?, 1953

*A*fter Colonel Nasser's assumption of power in Egypt in 1953, Anthony Eden, as Foreign Secretary, negotiated the withdrawal of British troops from the Suez Canal Zone. They were deployed instead in Cyprus. Eden, however, became progressively suspicious of Nasser's motives and believed that he was determined to undermine British interests in the key strategic area of the Middle East. This cartoon, by Illingworth, is based upon Tenniel's cartoon of Disraeli, who was rather more successful in dealing with the politics of the Canal.

A SHEEP IN WOLF'S CLOTHING, 1956

A cruel but fair cartoon by Leslie Illingworth. Eden was not suited to playing the sort of politics that would have taxed even Machiavelli.

16 · Things fall apart

PRIME MINISTERS
January 1957: Harold Macmillan (later Earl Stockton)
October 1963: Alec Douglas-Home (formerly Earl Home,
later Lord Home)
October 1964: Harold Wilson (later Lord Wilson)
June 1970: Edward Heath. *March 1974:* Harold Wilson (2nd Ministry)
April 1976–May 1979: James Callaghan
(later Lord Callaghan)

ANTHONY EDEN did not recommend a successor. After sounding out Tory MPs and consulting Churchill, the Queen chose Harold Macmillan, the Chancellor of the Exchequer, over the claims of R.A. Butler, who, many thought, would succeed.

Macmillan immediately set about restoring the morale of the Conservative Party. The style was the man. He had an air of Edwardian patrician grandeur; he did not conceal his liking for shooting parties, and for Trollope. All this concealed a consummate politician who rode a wave of economic success and declared, 'You've never had it so good.' To spread a little happiness, he deliberately introduced expansionist policies, which initiated the great postwar era of high inflation.

Macmillan healed the wounds of Suez and led the Tory Party to a third successive election victory in 1959. The cartoonists loved Macmillan, his moustache, his hair, his stiff demeanour, the old-fashioned clothes and the even older-fashioned cunning. As Prime Minister, he invented the photocall.

In foreign affairs, Macmillan cemented the special relationship with the United States, getting on particularly well with its new, young President, J.F. Kennedy. He presided over the liquidation of the Empire and prophetically told the South African Parliament to take heed of the 'Winds of Change' that were sweeping through Africa. But in 1963 he failed to get into the Common Market when his old wartime colleague, Charles de Gaulle, said 'Non'. After this, Macmillan lost much of his zest for governing. His last months were spent trying to stem the sleaze that flowed from the Profumo Affair. It was a sad end to his premiership.

SUPERMAC, 1958

Quintin Hogg, the Conservative Party Chairman, is saying to the Chancellor of the Exchequer, Derek Heathcoat-Amory, in the Box Office that their Leader was bringing the crowds back. Vicky had created the image of 'Supermac'. Contrary to his intention, 'Supermac' became a political legend, which helped Macmillan to increase his majority in the Election of 1959.

TWIST AND TWIST AND TWIST AGAIN, 1962

Ted Heath was a popular band leader in the 1960s, but another Ted Heath, the politician, was in charge of Britain's negotiations with the Common Market. In Vicky's band there are Iain McLeod, Rab Butler, Duncan Sandys and Selwyn Lloyd. They play the music of a new and popular dance, the Twist. This reflects the differing views in the Conservative Party over the Common Market and the need to adjust endlessly the position that Harold Macmillan took. All future leaders of the Conservative Party faced the same problem.

167

NO!, 1963

*I*n January 1963, General de Gaulle vetoed Britain's entry into the Common Market. This damaged the credibility of Harold Macmillan, and that of his Government, and he never really recovered from the setback. Cartoon by Leslie Illingworth.

I WONDER . . . WILL THEY STILL ACCEPT A CHEQUE?, 1963

*W*hen this cartoon by Cummings appeared in the Daily Express, Macmillan complained to the Political Editor. He resented the implication that his honour had been impugned by the sleaze of the time.

MACMILLAN CONFESSES, 1963

*T*he whole world of politics was convulsed in the summer of 1963 by a scandal between the War Minister, John Profumo, and a certain Christine Keeler. When he revealed that he had lied to the House of Commons about this affair, he had to resign. The cartoon by Gerald Scarfe was based on a famous photograph of the naked Christine Keeler straddling a modern chair.

Macmillan had appeared to be wordly-wise, but his handling of the scandal had been naive and gullible. Nigel Birch, a minister whom Macmillan had forced into resignation, made a devastating speech in the House in which he quoted the words from Robert Browning's poem, 'The Lost Leader' – 'Never glad confident morning again'. Macmillan slunk out of the Chamber knowing that he had come to the end of the road.

Gerald Scarfe drew first for the Daily Sketch *and the* Evening Standard, *but he really came into his own when he began to contribute to* Private Eye *from 1961. His cartoons are brutal and grotesque, and he reintroduced the savagery and explicitness of the 18th Century.*

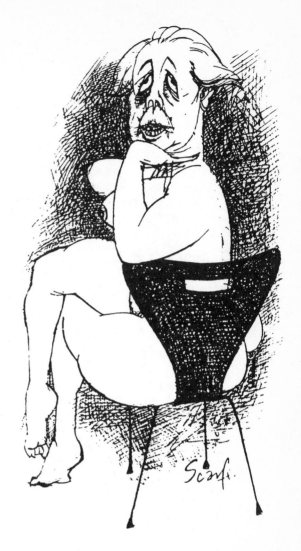

When Macmillan fell ill in 1963, the Tory Party was thrown into turmoil at its Conference in Blackpool, for a successor had to be chosen. Macmillan gave advice to the Queen from his hospital bed and, once again, he scuppered R.A. Butler by favouring the Earl of Home, the Foreign Secretary. The Peerage Act had just been passed and that allowed him to renounce his peerage and become Sir Alec Douglas-Home.

Alec Douglas-Home was a Godsend for the cartoonists. He was very thin, with a pointed face that was frequently transformed into a skull. He also wore half-moon glasses and these became the cartoonists' symbol for him.

"I hope ye're no' offended, Sir Alec—my wee bairns are a wee bit radically minded."

I HOPE YE'RE NO' OFFENDED, SIR ALEC, 1963

Although he first sat in the House of Commons in the 1930s and was Chamberlain's Parliamentary Secretary, much of Douglas-Home's life had been spent in the House of Lords. After he renounced his peerage, a seat had to be found for him in the House of Commons; George Younger, the candidate for a by-election in Kinross and West Perthshire, nobly stepped aside.

Giles' cartoons are usually social, rather than political, and his 'grandmother' has become one of the great cartoon figures of all time. On this rare occasion, he includes a Prime Minister.

THE MAN WHO NEVER WAS, 1965

Alec Douglas-Home only stayed on as Leader of the Conservative Party for a few months after his defeat in the 1964 Election. His successor, Ted Heath, was the first Leader of the Tory Party to be elected rather than to 'emerge'. Alec behaved as he had always done, impeccably. He was the epitome of loyalty and decency, and continued to be loved and respected by Party supporters. The artist is Vicky.

170 *Things Fall Apart*

VIETNAM, WILSON RIGHT BEHIND JOHNSON, 1965

Cartooning changed in the 1960s, largely because of Gerald Scarfe and Ralph Steadman. They both returned to the older Gillray style of rough and, at times, vulgar images. Punch *gentility was deliberately discarded – 'caricatura' returned with a vengeance. This was Scarfe's view of Harold Wilson's support of the Vietnam policy of the American President, L.B. Johnson. When the cartoon was first shown to the Editor of* Private Eye, *L.B.J.'s buttocks were bare. That, apparently, was too much for Mr Ingrams, who asked that some underpants be added.*

I'VE HEARD OF A SPECIAL RELATIONSHIP, BUT THIS IS RIDICULOUS

VIETNAM WILSON RIGHT BEHIND JOHNSON

Gerald Scarfe

Alec Douglas-Home, like Rosebery, had a bleak, wasting inheritance. The end of a long period of Conservative rule was approaching. He was a complete contrast to the Labour Leader, Harold Wilson. Home frankly admitted that, unlike Wilson who was at home with the 'white heat of the technological revolution', he preferred to sort out economic affairs with a box of matches. Although Home was not adept at the art of political in-fighting, he averted a Labour landslide, for Harold Wilson only won the October 1964 Election by four seats.

Harold Wilson had become Leader of the Labour Party in 1963 after the sudden and unexpected death of Hugh Gaitskell. He lashed the Conservatives for 'thirteen wasted years' and pledged to rejuvenate Britain with the politics of modernism. With a narrow majority he could not introduce many measures, though his Deputy, George Brown, did publish an ambitious National Plan. This optimistic, and unrealistic, prospectus helped Wilson to increase his majority in the 1966 Election. He boasted proudly that Labour had become the permanent Party of Government.

Wilson was, however, soon overwhelmed by economic and inflationary crises. Wages and prices were controlled by law; the pound was devalued in 1967; the country was racked by strikes. He attempted to reform industrial relations, but had to go personally to the House of Commons to withdraw his White Paper, 'In Place of Strife'. He gabbled

VAROOMSHKA, 1970

John Kent invented, in his cartoons for The Guardian, *a beautiful and scantily clad lady, Varoomshka, who was a commentator upon events. Here she pokes fun at Harold Wilson's preoccupation with imagined plots, as well as the way that he had been let down by his Cabinet colleagues, Callaghan and Jenkins, who are shown in this cartoon, and by the 'frugging Foreign Secretary', George Brown. Brown had resigned from Wilson's government in March 1968. The shadowy profile at the bottom was Michael Stewart, Brown's little-known successor as Foreign Secretary.*

Kent is yet another New Zealander and Varoomshka is based upon his wife, Nina. He describes her role as 'the permanent link between absurdities'.

through it, until one Tory MP called out, 'Eat them slow, Harold, eat them slow.' The unions had humiliated their Labour Prime Minister and Wilson muttered to the union leader, Hugh Scanlon, 'take your tanks off my lawn, Hughie'. By 1970, the great hopes of 1964 were shattered and, more than anything else, it was evident that a Labour Government could not control the trade unions.

The tabs of recognition for Wilson were his pipe and his quilted, padded Gannex coat, which was popular at the time. He only managed to keep the Labour Party together – no mean feat – by ingenious dexterity, which is depicted in cartoons as devious deceit. He was never allowed to forget his statement on TV after the devaluation crisis, 'The pound in your pocket will not be devalued.'

Edward Heath had succeeded Alec Douglas-Home as Conservative Leader in 1965. He was the first person to be elected to that position. He, too, came to office with a programme to revitalize the economy, based upon market forces, less state intereference, and union reform. This was

172 Things Fall Apart

SQUARING UP, 1970

*T*he double act that emerged in the
1960s and 1970s was Wilson
versus Heath. It never quite acquired
the status of Pitt and Fox, or Disraeli
and Gladstone.

John Jensen, yet another cartoonist
from Australia, settled in London in
1950. He has drawn social and
political cartoons for many newspapers
and magazines, including the New
Statesman *and – in this case – in the*
Sunday Telegraph.

THE CHARGE OF THE LIGHT
BRIGADE, 1974

*T*his prophetic cartoon by
Cummings predicted that Ted
Heath's decision to call the Election of
1974 was foolhardy and doomed. Ted
advances into battle, flanked by Willie
Whitelaw and Tony Barber, against the
massed ranks of the Labour Party led
by Harold Wilson, the Liberals led by

Jeremy Thorpe, and by Enoch Powell
who had resigned from the
Conservative Party and had urged
Conservatives to vote Labour. They are
ranged alongside the leaders of the
National Union of Mineworkers. It
was a disastrous campaign, in which
the Tory lead was eroded by leaks from
the Wages Board and by attacks from
industrialists.

Things Fall Apart 173

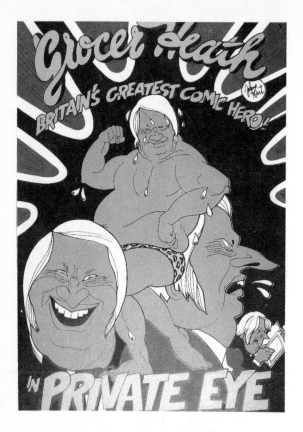

GROCER HEATH, 1973

Ted Heath was given the title, 'Grocer', when he was Britain's principal negotiator for entry to the Common Market in 1961–62. It stuck. Cartoon by John Kent.

the essence of the famous Selsdon Park Manifesto (1970), but within two years it was abandoned. The unions once again showed their power and when, in 1972, miners received a 17 per cent pay award, Ted Heath executed a massive U-turn and introduced statutory control of wages, prices, rents and dividends. He then decided to try to run the country by a form of corporatism in which the leaders of industry and the trade unions agreed policy with him at No. 10. It didn't work.

Ted Heath was a gift to the cartoonists. His props were his sailing boat and his conductor's baton. Figuratively, they concentrated on his long, sharp nose, his teeth, his switch-on and switch-off smile, and his obesity.

Domestically, Heath's Government achieved little, but he will be remembered for taking Britain into the Common Market in 1972. The nature of Britain's relationship with Europe was to overshadow the next twenty-five years; it was to be for the Tories as great an issue as Free Trade in the 1840s and Tariff Reform in the early 1900s.

The inevitable rigidities of a prices and incomes policy led to another miners' strike in the autumn of 1973. Industry was reduced to working three days a week; ration books for petrol were issued. The country

FINAL APPEARANCE – OR GRAND COMEBACK, 1974

*A*fter *his narrow victory in February 1974, Wilson called another election in October. Heath had continued to lead the Conservative Party, hoping for a comeback. After his defeat in October, his leadership was increasingly challenged. In February 1975 he resigned after he had come second to Margaret Thatcher in the first round of the Tory leadership ballot.*

Wally Fawkes (Trog) was born in Canada. He had his first chance at the Daily Mail *at the end of the Second World War. His cartoons have appeared in many magazines and papers, notably since 1965 in* The Observer. *He also drew several memorable covers for* Punch, *of which this is one.*

seemed near to collapse and in February 1974 Heath held a General Election on the question of 'Who Governs Britain?' The country clearly decided that it was not going to be Ted Heath. The Tories ended up with a smaller number of seats than Labour and for a few days Heath tried to get the Liberals, led by Jeremy Thorpe, to form a coalition. When that effort collapsed, the Queen sent for Harold Wilson again.

Wilson had just scraped home. Repeating the success of the 1960s, he held another Election in October 1974 and increased his majority. When he resigned in 1976, Jim Callaghan was elected by the Labour Party in his place. By that time, Labour's majority had all but disappeared. Unable to get through further nationalization measures in 1976, he formed an informal Alliance with David Steel, the Leader of the Liberal Party. This Lib/Lab pact kept him in office for another three years.

The cartoonists were, on the whole, kind to Callaghan. He was known as 'Sunny Jim' and sometimes depicted as a farmer since he had some land in Sussex. He had no striking physical characteristics and he was dubbed 'The Prime Minister of Dock Green' after the popular television show, *Dixon of Dock Green*, in which Jack Warner played the friendly neighbourhood bobby.

Things Fall Apart 175

DO WE ALL SELL OUT IN THE END?, 1976

Scarfe savagely comments upon Wilson receiving the Garter on his resignation. Wilson surprised many by announcing his resignation in March 1976. It was assumed that there was some devious motive behind it, but apparently he had agreed with his wife that he would resign at that time, and he had previously announced, though few believed him, that he intended to retire at the age of sixty. It was a remarkable event, for he had a good working majority, his Party would not have ditched him and he was still very much in the political swim.

Jim Callaghan decided not to hold a General Election in the Autumn of 1978, though he would probably have won. He then had to go through 'The Winter of Discontent', when the trade unions made the Government massively unpopular – hospitals were closed, rubbish piled up in the streets, the dead were left unburied.

In January 1979, returning from a conference in the Caribbean, Callaghan complacently gave the impression that everything was alright. 'Crisis, what crisis?', summed it up. Although he never actually used those words, they dogged him.

In the General Election in May, Margaret Thatcher set out new policies to revive the country, based upon monetarism and market forces. In the campaign, she made maximum use of Labour's unpopularity. The Tories displayed a poster with a long queue of unemployed people and the slogan, 'Labour isn't Working'. Callaghan himself believed that his defeat was due to a change in the political tides which he could not resist.

DAVID AND JIMLIETH, 1978

*I*n 1978, towards the end of the
*Lib/Lab Pact, David Steel, the
Leader of the Liberal Party, announced
that Liberal support would be
withdrawn at the end of the
Parliament. The Government fell in
May 1979 when the Scottish
Nationalists, who had also been
supporting Labour, decided to vote
against them on a censure motion. This*

act was correctly described by
Callaghan as 'turkeys voting for an
early Christmas'. When the Liberals
deserted Labour, Michael Foot, in a
devastating speech, dubbed Steel as
'the boy David'.

Les Gibbard, also from New
Zealand, came to London in 1967 and
was The Guardian's main political
cartoonist from 1969 to 1994. His
drawings are not cruel and tell the
political story without malice.

THE PLUM PUDDING IN
DANGER, 1979

*T*his cartoon by Jensen appeared
*after Callaghan's defeat in May
1979. The fight was on for the soul of
the Labour Party. Here, Tony Benn
lays his claim for the 'Left'. Michael
Foot, another left-wing figure, became
Leader of the Labour Party in 1981.
Several prominent former Cabinet
Ministers broke away to form the
Social Democrats. The plum pudding
had been carved up.*

Things Fall Apart 177

17 · Thatcher and Major

PRIME MINISTERS
May 1979: Margaret Thatcher (later Baroness Thatcher)
November 1990–: John Major

MARGARET THATCHER broke with the postwar consensus of Butskellism, Heath's corporatism and the Wilson-Callaghan income policies. All these had failed to produce non-inflationary growth, coupled with harmonious industrial relations. A new approach was needed.

To break the inflationary spiral, started by Harold Macmillan, sound money became the prime target. At the low point of the recession, Geoffrey Howe, in his 1981 Budget, cut expenditure and supported a strong pound. Although 364 economists condemned this policy, to Margaret Thatcher it was the foundation stone of the economic success of the 1980s. Cutting income tax was also a central pillar of Thatcherism.

The major constitutional change that Margaret Thatcher made was to curb the power of the trade union bosses. In her view, the trade unions had become a separate estate of the realm; they sought to share No. 10 Downing Street with the Prime Ministers, from whichever political party they came. The leading left-wing trade union leader, Arthur Scargill, took on Margaret in a year-long miners' strike. She didn't budge, and her victory marked the end of prolonged trade union power.

In 1982, the Falklands War made Margaret Thatcher a world figure. Against most expectations and odds, Britain launched a fleet; the Islands were recaptured from the Argentinians. Michael Foot, the Leader of the Labour Party, supported her; as for him, it was a crusade against a fascist dictator.

Margaret Thatcher came to enjoy playing a major role in world politics; because of her personality, Britain boxed in a class above its weight. She revelled in the title given to her by the Russians in 1976 – 'The Iron Lady'. She quickly appreciated the importance of Gorbachev and supported his reforms. She became a symbol of freedom in many Eastern European countries which wanted to break away from Soviet hegemony.

COLOSSUS, 1985

*T*he dichotomy in Thatcherism. On the one side are the liberalizers who wanted less state control; on the other, there are those Ministers, including me, who had unhappily to use the Courts to impose Treasury policy on local authorities.

Thatcherism failed to establish a suitable relationship between local and central government.

This cartoon is by Richard Willson, who has drawn many realistic cartoons, principally for The Times, *though this one appeared as a front cover for the Tory magazine,* Crossbow.

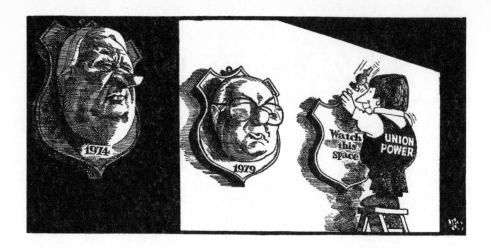

WATCH THIS SPACE, 1979

*B*oth Ted Heath and Jim Callaghan had been brought down by the abuse of trade union power. Margaret Thatcher was determined that she was not going to be the third trophy. One of her first priorities was to set in train a series of reforms that reduced the power of organized trade unions, but in some respects enhanced the rights of individual trade unionists. She also made clear to the Trades Union Council that she was not prepared to share the government of the country with them. Cartoon by Trog (Wally Fawkes).

THE IRON LADY, 1981

*T*he Russians dubbed Margaret Thatcher 'The Iron Lady' as early as 1976. Ted Heath has said of the title, 'It was the biggest mistake the Russians ever made. They thought it would damn her. It did exactly the opposite.'

Steve Bell is a socialist who has drawn for the New Statesman and The Guardian since 1981. He thought Margaret Thatcher was demented and tried to show this in the way he drew her eyes. He is essentially a comic-strip artist who draws in very fine detail.

IN THE LAND OF NO U-TURNS, 1980

*A*t the Conservative Party Conference in 1980, Margaret Thatcher defiantly said, 'The lady's not for turning'; with this single phrase she saw off many of her critics on the left of the Tory Party who were dubbed the Wets. She remembered being in Ted Heath's Cabinet in 1972 when he made a massive U-turn in economic policy; she was determined not to make the same mistake. 'No U-turns', and its sister, 'TINA – There Is No Alternative', became her hallmarks.

Ralph Steadman turns Margaret Thatcher's hair and face into a traffic signal. This is a good example of a cartoon playing to the target's strengths.

Steadman started cartooning in the late 1950s and has drawn for many magazines and newspapers. His anger with politicians of all parties characterizes his best – and most brutal – work. He is also a prolific book illustrator.

FRILLY KNICKERS, 1981

*B*ill Deedes, the editor of the Daily Telegraph, *refused to publish this cartoon by Nicholas Garland. Garland wanted to show that the Iron Lady had acted out of character by approving some defence cuts – hence the frilly knickers. Deedes defended his decision on the grounds that an editor has to decide what will be acceptable to his readers. He believed that many Daily Telegraph readers would have been offended by this cartoon. 'It was the knickers', he said, adding with a chuckle, 'The iron skirt was a bit short too.'*

THERE AREN'T ENOUGH WOMEN IN MY CABINET!, 1982

*T*his Cummings cartoon appeared in the Daily Express *just after the start of the Falklands War and after the resignation of Margaret Thatcher's* Foreign Secretary, Lord Carrington, and of his deputy, Humphrey Atkins. Margaret Thatcher's domination of her Cabinet was a fairly regular theme for cartoonists. This played to her strength, for Prime Ministers do not mind if they are portrayed as being powerful, decisive and in charge.

THE FALKLANDS WAR, 1982

*B*efore 1982, most Britons would probably have had difficulty in placing the Falklands on the map. That deficiency in education was made good in April 1982 when Argentina invaded the islands, which they called the Malvinas, to claim them as their territory. Such a challenge was made for the iron will of Margaret Thatcher. Before a sceptical, but then a largely admiring world, she despatched a fleet and an army to recover the Falklands. Overnight she became a world figure who counted. Before, the Government had been trailing in the polls, heading for electoral defeat; but afterwards, in the Election of 1983, Margaret Thatcher increased her majority.

ALL THE OLD JOKES TOGETHER, 1986

*N*ot even in Queen Victoria's time were the Prime Minister and five Prime Ministerial predecessors all living at the same time. Photograph from Private Eye.

STRONG MEDICINE, 1987

*T*he Conservative Manifesto for the 1987 General Election was the most radical of the Thatcher years. It committed the Party to a comprehensive reform of education, a new housing policy and the introduction of a community charge.

In the General Election campaign, Labour did not focus on the community charge, but when it became the 'Poll Tax', it came to dominate the politics of 1989–90.

Kal, a Canadian cartoonist, drew principally for the Economist, *although this cartoon appeared in the* Today *newspaper.*

SPITTING IMAGE, 1987

*F*luck and Law created their rubber
puppets for the television series
Spitting Image. *Their heyday was the
middle of the Thatcher years,
1985–88. They made several puppets
of Margaret Thatcher, but all
emphasized her masculine qualities,
and probably more people laughed
with her than at her.*

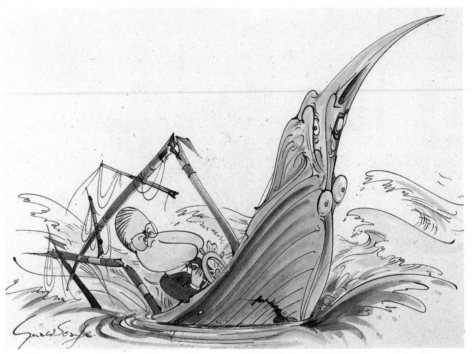

GOING DOWN WITH THE SHIP, 1990

I was the Party Chairman at the time
of Margaret Thatcher's fall. Not only
did I support her to the end – being
one of the few Cabinet Ministers who
urged her to stand in the second round
of the leadership election – but I also
did what I could to prevent the Party
falling apart at a time when loyalties
were strained. In the leadership
election in November, Michael
Heseltine secured sufficient votes in the
first round to bring about Margaret
Thatcher's resignation. In the second
round, John Major came from the back
and won.

THE FALL OF MARGARET THATCHER, 1990

*S*teve Bell's funeral procession is headed by Michael Heseltine, wearing his Tarzan loincloth. Geoffrey Howe, who played the role of chief assassin with his devastating speech in the House of Commons, is depicted as a sheep.

Europe was one of the issues that brought down Margaret Thatcher. She fought off pressure from Nigel Lawson, the Chancellor of the Exchequer, and Geoffrey Howe, her Foreign Secretary, to join the ERM. She became increasingly opposed to the centralist tendencies of the European Union, and advocated a 'Europe de Patries'. Both Lawson and Howe resigned over Europe and this played a part in her losing the leadership election in November 1990. The Government was then going through a period of great unpopularity, which had been exacerbated by the first year of the Poll Tax. Some Conservative MPs believed that Margaret Thatcher should have resigned on her tenth anniversary in 1989; enough of them lost their bottle and voted to sack her.

The 1980s were the Thatcher Decade. Economic decline was halted; Britain walked tall; and Margaret Thatcher won three General Elections in a row, 1979, 1983 and 1987. As she proudly said, 'I was never defeated or rejected by the British people.'

Margaret Thatcher's successor was John Major, whose ascent to the premiership was almost as speedy as Stanley Baldwin's, for only seven years earlier he had been a backbencher. Anyone following Margaret Thatcher was going to have a very difficult time. Comparisons were made and they were bound to be unfavourable.

The period up to the General Election of 1992 was like a long honeymoon. Although all the polls indicated that the Tories would lose, John Major was not dispirited. He campaigned vigorously and won a narrow victory. That was the high point of his premiership, for soon after a series of calamitous events precipitated a period of unrelenting decline in his Government's fortunes.

THERE'S A BREATHLESS HUSH IN THE CLOSE TONIGHT, 1991

*M*argaret Thatcher was strongly opposed to the Maastricht negotiations, which were conducted in 1991. Her presence in the background was a constant source of difficulty for John Major. Cartoonists have focused on John Major's passionate interest in cricket; bat, ball, wicket and pads have all been frequently used to capture a particular event, as in this example by Garland.

SUPERMAN, 1991

*S*teve Bell had first caricatured John Major as a turnip, one of the vegetables on Maggie's Farm, then as a poodle, but neither worked. Subsequently, he hit on the idea of depicting him as a naff superman. Superman's bright red trunks were replaced by Marks and Spencer airtex Y-fronts, which were worn outside his trousers. They have become John Major's badge in Bell cartoons.

Alastair Campbell, now the Press Officer for Tony Blair, but at the time a political journalist, claimed that on a trip with John Major overseas, he noticed that the edge of Major's underpants protruded above his trousers. This indicated to Campbell that the Prime Minister tucked his shirt into his underpants. Campbell claims authorship for the idea, but Steve Bell says that it only confirms his own image of the Prime Minister. Anyway, it stuck.

186 *Thatcher and Major*

THE SOAP BOX, 1992

In the General Election of 1992, the polls all indicated that the Tories were going to be well and truly beaten. Knowing that the campaign was going badly, John Major abandoned the plans that his Party Chairman, Chris Patten, had made. He used a soap box to stand on at his open-air meetings. This caught the imagination of the

country, transformed the campaign and led to one of the few favourable cartoons of John Major. Against the odds, he beat Neil Kinnock, the leader of the Labour Party, who confidently expected to be swept into No. 10.

The cartoon is by Peter Brookes, who started to draw political cartoons for The Times *in 1991. He has one of the most acute political minds among contemporary cartoonists.*

The clumsy announcement of pit closures caused the first Tory back-benchers' rebellion. One member of the Cabinet, David Mellor, was forced to resign over a much-publicized affair with an actress, the first of several resignations over 'sleaze'. In September 1992, after a day of financial turmoil and humiliation, Britain had to abandon its membership of the ERM, which John Major as Chancellor of the Exchequer had entered. From then on it was politically downhill. Ironically, the same moment marked the beginning of the country's economic recovery.

In 1993, the Government had to take a Bill through the House of Commons to implement the Maastricht Treaty negotiated by Major in

Thatcher and Major 187

ADORATION OF THE MAJOR, 1992

John Major's honeymoon, after his success in the 1992 General Election, was very short. Things started to go wrong in the summer. David Mellor, one of the Prime Minister's closest confidantes, had to resign when it was revealed he was having an affair with an actress who alleged that he had made love to her wearing a Chelsea football shirt. Mellor is shown on the right. The basic problem was still Europe and Norman Tebbit emerged as the Prime Minister's principal critic, seen here gnawing at his leg. By that time, Margaret Thatcher had become convinced that the Maastricht Treaty reduced Britain's sovereignty considerably.

If this cartoon had appeared in the 19th Century, or even in the 18th Century, it would have been considered blasphemous and the cartoonist would probably have been prosecuted. Now, there wasn't a whisper.

'Surely, John, you wouldn't want to see an end to age-old British customs like this...?'

SURELY JOHN, 1992

This is a time-honoured process that Prime Ministers follow. The only one who did not in recent years – and he is not shown in this cartoon – is Alec Douglas-Home, whose conduct towards his successor, Ted Heath, was exemplary and very rare. Cartoon by Stan McMurtry.

WILL HE FALL?, 1993

At the time of the Conservative Party Conference in 1993, it looked as if John Major's leadership would be challenged that Autumn. It wasn't, and he didn't fall.

This cartoon also shows how difficult it was for anyone to fill Margaret Thatcher's shoes. Chris Riddell works principally for The Independent *and the* Economist; *his very detailed cartoons are finely drawn.*

1991. This produced running warfare between the Eurosceptics and the Government. The Bill was only passed when John Major put his own leadership on the line during the Summer of 1993. By 1994, the balance of opinion in the Conservative Party had shifted to being Eurosceptic.

John Major has been harshly treated by cartoonists. Margaret Thatcher had a rough time at their hands, too, but she was portrayed as a strong figure, albeit spiky. She was a conviction politician, he is a consensus politician.

The cartoonists have been unrelenting in their depiction of him as indecisive, grey, stubborn and hapless. His personal success in Northern Ireland and in securing the economic recovery were either ignored or attributed to factors beyond his control. The press and cartoonists have hunted him like a pack of hounds in pursuit of a fox. Some have attacked him because he is not like Thatcher, whilst others have attacked him for continuing to pursue Thatcherite policies. It says much for John Major's resilience that – at the time of writing – he has decided to continue as Leader of the Conservative Party and as Prime Minister. He is confident that the Muse of History will be kinder to him and his record than some of his contemporaries.

191

192